The Art of Learning to Teach
to Teach
Creating Professional Narratives

Second Edition

Mary Beattie
**Ontario Institute for Studies in Education
University of Toronto**

PEARSON

Merrill
Prentice Hall

Upper Saddle River, New Jersey
Columbus, Ohio

Library of Congress Cataloging-in-Publication Data

Beattie, Mary
    The art of learning to teach: creating professional narratives/
    Mary Beattie.—2nd ed.
    p. cm.
    Includes bibliographical references.
    ISBN 0-13-174769-X
    1. Student teachers—Biography. 2. Student teaching. I. Title.

LB2157.A3B39 2006
370.71′1—dc22

                         2006042000

Vice President and Executive Publisher: Jeffery W. Johnston
Executive Editor: Debra A. Stollenwerk
Senior Editorial Assistant: Mary Morrill
Production Editor: Kris Roach
Production Coordination: Sharon Montooth, Michael Bass & Associates
Design Coordinator: Diane C. Lorenzo
Art and Cover Design: Jason Moore
Production Manager: Susan Hannahs
Director of Marketing: David Gesell
Senior Marketing Manager: Darcy Betts Prybella
Marketing Coordinator: Brian Mounts

This book was set in Palatino by Integra Software Services. It was printed
and bound by R.R. Donnelley & Sons Company. The cover was printed by
R.R. Donnelley & Sons Company.

Pearson Education Ltd.   Pearson Education Australia Pty. Limited
Pearson Education Singapore Pte. Ltd. Pearson Education North Asia Ltd.
Pearson Education Canada, Ltd.   Pearson Educación de Mexico, S.A. de C.V.
Pearson Education—Japan   Pearson Education Malaysia Pte. Ltd.

10 9 8 7 6 5 4 3 2 1
ISBN: 0-13-174769-X

Life must be lived forwards, but it can only be understood backwards.

Kierkegaard

This book is about professional learning in the context of becoming a teacher and of learning to teach. The journey you are about to begin will engage you in reflection and inquiry where you will explore what you have learned from your life experiences. You will learn to articulate what you know and use it to learn what you need to know. Throughout this learning journey, you will be encouraged to explore the values, beliefs, and assumptions which inform your actions and practices, and examine them in the light of new insights and understandings. You will document the details of your reflections and ongoing inquiry, and eventually write a narrative of professional learning that is unique to the person you are and to the professional teacher you want to become. Your narrative will provide insights into your learning and unlearning, your methods of reflection and inquiry, and your ways of creating an ethically based professional knowledge in teaching. It will also show the person and the personality behind the ideas and issues, and provide insights into your learning processes, your beliefs and theories of teaching and learning, your passions and preoccupations, and your hopes and dreams.

The narratives you read throughout the book will present you with the details of the learning journeys taken by other beginning teachers. These narratives will stimulate your reflections and inquiry as you read about the ways in which each of these individuals learned to question, to make connections, and to create a professional knowledge that was uniquely theirs. They show how the personal and professional are connected in their lives, and how learning involves the whole person— the intellectual, emotional, social, moral, aesthetic, and spiritual aspects of the person who is becoming a teacher. Their narratives also show how making connections and relationships is a central aspect of creating a professional knowledge in teaching—the relationship between all aspects of the person who is becoming a teacher, between the self and others, between practice and theory, between past experience and future goals, and between the way things are and the way they might be.

You will read about the ways in which these beginning teachers used the inquiry process to explore the ways in which they have learned throughout their lives, to learn about difference and diversity among students, and to learn to teach in ways that would enhance all students' learning. Their narratives provide insights into the ways in which they learned about students' interests, about their diverse learning styles, backgrounds, and purposes. They also show how they searched for teaching strategies and classroom procedures that would engage students more fully in the learning process and would inspire them to participate in the curriculum of the classroom in authentic and personally meaningful ways. As you read through these narratives of professional learning, you will read about significant experiences of learning and unlearning, and of how the processes of reflection and inquiry enabled these beginning teachers to understand their roles in the context of a quest for the good, and of making a difference not only in their classrooms, but in their schools and in society. In so doing, they created a strong correspondence between their methods of inquiry, their reflective processes and teaching practices, and those espoused in current pedagogical theory, in research and professional journals, in methods classes, and in professional discussions.

The narratives and activities throughout the book are designed to help you to explore the complexities of becoming a teacher and of learning to teach. They will help you to recognize your strengths and to use them to learn what you need to know, to develop your unique voice, and to learn how to hear the voices of others. They are also designed to help you to deal with the complexities and difficulties of creating an authentic professional identity, developing meaningful relationships with students and colleagues, and fostering democratic learning communities in your classroom and school.

The narratives are written in beginning teachers' own voices, in their own language, and in forms that allowed them to focus on their particular priorities and perspectives. These individuals come from a range of academic and cultural backgrounds and represent different age groups. They all came to the teacher education program with an undergraduate degree in the arts, humanities, or sciences. Some had just recently completed their undergraduate degrees; others had left jobs and careers to embark on a career in teaching. Their narratives were written in the context of the teacher education program where they were enrolled as a cohort in two consecutive courses in the foundations of education: (a) Developing a Personal Philosophy and (b) Teaching: Students, Schools, and Systems.

In the context of these two courses, individuals worked on a variety of activities, assignments, and projects that engaged them in the following:

- Individual and collaborative inquiry
- Ongoing reflective writing
- Exploration and sharing of metaphors and images of teaching and learning
- Role-play and simulation activities
- Analysis of critical incidents in practice
- Storytelling
- Cooperative and group presentations

These activities and their ongoing reflections and inquiry provided individuals with multiple opportunities to explore their own beliefs and understandings, to share ideas with others, to hear views and perspectives different to their own, and to create a professional knowledge in teaching.

As you read their narratives, you will hear the voices of practitioners who write, and not those of trained writers. Individually and collectively, these narratives acknowledge the interconnectedness of the mind and the body, the emotions and the intellect, and the spirit and the senses, in the process of becoming a teacher and of learning to teach. Here, *spirit* or *spiritual* is understood in a secular way, referring to a nonmaterial source of meaning in an individual's life. Each narrative provides insights into the unique journey taken by each individual who is drawing from a unique set of past experiences and has his or her own unique dreams and goals for the future. The individual narratives present the particular complexities and processes of inquiry that are distinctive to that individual and into the way in which new experiences, conversations, interaction, and collaboration enabled that individual to expand his or her knowledge, range of practices, perspectives, and worldviews. Collectively, they provide insights into the ways in which these beginning teachers came to recognize the necessity to create classroom communities that are based in the experiences and realities of the learner rather than those of the teacher. They also show how individuals learned to teach for student engagement and student success, and address common issues that face every prospective teacher: the differences between how they were taught and the ways in which they must teach, between what they themselves have experienced and what their students have experienced and are experiencing, between the kinds of schools they attended themselves and those in which they teach, and between the beginning teachers they are and the professional teachers they want to become.

Individually and collectively, the narratives are testimony to the complexities of becoming a teacher, to the joys and difficulties associated with the recognition that one's individual views and learning styles are valid but are not universally shared, and to the importance of on-going reflection, questioning, and self-directed inquiry in professional learning. They are a testament to the profoundly human endeavor of becoming a teacher, an endeavor that engages each person intellectually, emotionally, socially, physically, morally, and spiritually. They bear witness to the ways in which professional learning is a journey that links the individual's past, present, and future in profoundly intimate and human ways.

THE PHILOSOPHY OF THE TEXT

The philosophy of this text is based on a holistic and narrative approach to teaching and learning. It is understood that teacher education is based in inquiry, which is focused on the development of the whole person who is becoming a teacher. This involves the development of self-knowledge, knowledge of others, and knowledge of working collaboratively with others in classrooms, schools, and communities. It is acknowledged that becoming a teacher and learning to teach are inextricably intertwined and that professional learning is grounded in the individual's past experiences, current purposes, and future aspirations. It is also understood that individuals construct meaning from their interpretations of their experiences and reconstruct their knowledge in the light of new experiences, insights, and understandings.

Prospective teachers bring a wealth of prior experience, personal knowledge, and understanding to the professional learning situation, which provides them with a rich resource for reflection and inquiry. This knowledge, most of which has been gained as a student, must be examined and reconstructed in the context of becoming a teacher and in the creation of a professional knowledge of teaching. By reflecting on one's own experience, and through discussions and conversation with others, the individual develops his or her voice and expands it through hearing the insights and understandings of others. This philosophical perspective is grounded in Dewey's (1966) notion that we learn from experience and reflection on experience and that the "educational process is one of continual reorganizing, reconstructing, transforming experience" (p. 50). The goal of this kind of teacher education is to enable beginning teachers to reorganize and reconstruct their personal knowledge into a professional knowledge of teaching by providing many opportunities for reflecting on prior and current experiences, for considering and adapting what is known through listening to the perspectives of a variety of others, for stimulating new ways of thinking, and for developing the practices, habits, and capacities for ongoing reflection, inquiry, and meaning making.

This conceptual framework can be outlined in these three major themes:

- Teacher education is a holistic enterprise grounded in relationships, involving the whole person, and based in the context of the individual's whole life.
- Learning is a process of creation and re-creation, of learning from and with others, by continually adapting what is known in the light of what is learned.
- Stories and narratives are primary ways of thinking and knowing and of representing what is known. We understand our experience, our realities, and our journeys through life in the form of narratives that have beginnings, middles, and endings. The expansion of our understanding, perspectives, and worldviews involves us in the rescripting of these narratives and those of our community and of the world around us.

In the context of professional learning, these themes translate into the following principles of teaching and learning:

- The processes of learning to teach and of becoming a teacher are inextricably intertwined, and all aspects of the person—cognitive, social, moral, aesthetic, emotional, spiritual, and physical—are interrelated in the learning and in the teaching processes.
- Inquiry provides a central organizing framework for professional learning and for the continuous construction of a professional knowledge in teaching throughout an individual's career.
- The ability to reflect on experience and to learn from it is an essential aspect of becoming an ethically based professional. The continuous use and development of reflective abilities, habits, and practices are essential for a career of ethically based practice.
- Teaching and learning are relational endeavors, and professional learning is grounded in learning from oneself and from and with others. Within collaborative relationships with students and colleagues, professional teachers can achieve both personal and collectively constructed goals and work together to create authentic learning communities in their classrooms and schools.
- Professional learning begins in the examination of practice, of experience, and of the stories we enact in our lives, our schools, and our society. It involves understanding one's own story, learning to hear and understand the stories of others, and continuously rescripting the stories of self as teacher and of school, community, and society. Rescripting the story is about inventing the future, about imagining how things can be otherwise, and about working with colleagues to bring about a better world for all people.

THE GOAL OF THE TEXT

The goal of the text is to help teachers to create and re-create their professional knowledge through reflection and inquiry. Readers will have the opportunity to examine and consider a variety of possible responses to teaching and learning situations, and to relate their thinking to their own experience and developing professional knowledge. Readers will be invited to reflect and respond individually and collaboratively to what they read, and to document their reflections, responses, and ongoing inquiry. In this way teachers can use what they learn to build their own unique professional knowledge in teaching, and to plan their future actions and professional practices. The narratives serve as springboards for discussion, conversations, and self-conscious reflection on the nature and development of ethically based professionals. They provide rich resources for readers as they explore the stories of their own lives, open themselves up to the stories of others, and prepare to document the details of their professional learning.

SPECIAL FEATURES OF THE TEXT

The text encourages and guides the reader through the processes of reflection, inquiry, and the creation of a narrative of professional learning. It contains a variety of narratives written by beginning teachers who describe the unique journeys they took in the process of becoming professional teachers. These narratives are written in beginning teachers' own language, and they reflect their individual voices, purposes, perspectives, and realities. Individually and collectively, they show the unique processes by which these authors created authentic professional identities, developed professional relationships with students and colleagues, and worked to establish inquiry-based, democratic classrooms and schools. The narratives are followed by a wide range of suggested reflective activities and writing that prompt the reader to gain insights from the narratives themselves, and to relate them to their own experiences and situations. By building up a body of reflective writing over time in response to the chapters, the reader has a rich data bank from which to draw in order to create a narrative of his or her own professional learning.

The text has three major sections within which the narratives have been arranged according to the author's major focus:

1. Creating a Professional Identity: Connecting the Personal and the Professional
2. Creating Relationships and Making New Relations: Learning from and with Others

3. Creating New Narratives: Connecting Self, School, and Society
   - Each of these parts begins with an introduction to the theme and an overview of the narratives contained in the section.
   - Each narrative is introduced and the significant dimensions of the theme are highlighted.
   - Questions following each narrative invite the reader to reflect on and to respond to the ideas, the experiences, the meanings made, and the lessons learned. These questions are designed to stimulate thought, discussion, conversations, reflective writing, and professional action.
   - Suggested writing activities are included in the follow-up to each narrative. These ideas are designed to help beginning teachers document the details of their own professional learning. They are intended to provide support for the beginning teacher's developing voice and to stimulate and deepen the ongoing inquiry.
   - The introduction, "Letter from One Teacher to Another," presents the process of inquiry and the invitation to begin a portfolio of writing that documents the professional journey.
   - Chapter 13 is designed to support the writing of a professional narrative.

SUGGESTIONS FOR USING THE TEXT

Narratives of professional learning can be used by beginning teachers in teacher education programs. It is also designed to be used in graduate programs by experienced teachers as a resource for self-directed inquiry. The book will also be useful to associate teachers, curriculum and staff development consultants, teacher educators, and all those interested in the development of professional knowledge in teaching. The text can also be useful to those who are interested in holistic and narrative approaches to educational research, practitioner inquiry, and research that represents practitioners' voices. It is hoped that the reader will use the text in the way that best fits his or her particular purposes and interests by proceeding through the chapters as they are presented or by creating an alternate sequence better suited to the purpose at hand.

ACKNOWLEDGMENTS

I would like to express my gratitude to the many people who have made this book possible and who have helped me to realize the dream of a second edition. First and foremost, I want to thank my former students at the Ontario Institute for Studies in Education at The University of Toronto (DISE/UT) without whose contributions the book would not exist: Wendy Barber, Gilbert Barsky, Alicia Cashore, George Haddad, Steven Hunt, Doug Kirkaldy, Carol Sapiano, Ellen Shifrin, Doug Stratford and Ruth Weinstock. These voices have inspired me as I worked on the first and second editions of the book.

I also want to thank the publishing team at Merrill/Prentice Hall for their support throughout this project. I am especially grateful to Debbie Stollenwerk, whose guidance and wisdom have been so valuable to me from the beginning. Sharon Montooth, the Production Editor, and Laura Larson of Leap for Words have provided their special expertise to the copyediting and layout of the book.

I would like to express my gratitude to the reviewers who provided such excellent feedback on the first edition of the text. They are Paula D. Packer, Lock Haven University of Pennsylvania; Michael Perl, Kansas State University; Theresa S. Stewart, University of Illinois—Springfield; and Duncan Waite, Texas State University, San Marcos. I have responded to their comments and suggestions throughout the chapters, and I believe this has helped me to create a better book. Foremost among the changes in this second edition is a re-written and expanded version of Chapter 13, Writing a Narrative, where I have tried to provide more support and practical suggestions for the writing.

Finally, I want to express my deep gratitude to my husband Jim, whose love and encouragement always feels like a blessing. I owe him more than I can say.

Mary Beattie

Teacher Preparation Classroom

TEACHER PREP

MERRILL
PRENTICE HALL

Your Class. Their Careers. Our Future. Will your students be prepared?
We invite you to explore our new, innovative and engaging website and all that it has to offer you, your course, and tomorrow's educators! Organized around the major courses pre-service teachers take, the Teacher Preparation site provides media, student/teacher artifacts, strategies, research articles, and other resources to equip your students with the quality tools needed to excel in their courses and prepare them for their first classroom.

This ultimate on-line education resource is available at no cost, when packaged with a Merrill text, and will provide you and your students access to:

Online Video Library. More than 150 video clips—each tied to a course topic and framed by learning goals and Praxis-type questions—capture real teachers and students working in real classrooms, as well as in-depth interviews with both students and educators.

Student and Teacher Artifacts. More than 200 student and teacher classroom artifacts—each tied to a course topic and framed by learning goals and application questions—provide a wealth of materials and experiences to help make your study to become a professional teacher more concrete and hands-on.

Research Articles. Over 500 articles from ASCD's renowned journal *Educational Leadership*. The site also includes Research Navigator, a searchable database of additional educational journals.

Teaching Strategies. Over 500 strategies and lesson plans for you to use when you become a practicing professional.

Licensure and Career Tools. Resources devoted to helping you pass your licensure exam; learn standards, law, and public policies; plan a teaching portfolio; and succeed in your first year of teaching.

How to ORDER *Teacher Prep* for you and your students:
For students to receive a *Teacher Prep* Access Code with this text, instructors **must** provide a special value pack ISBN number on their textbook order form. To receive this special ISBN, please email: **Merrill.marketing@pearsoned.com** and provide the following information:
- Name and Affiliation
- Author/Title/Edition of Merrill text
Upon ordering *Teacher Prep* for their students, instructors will be given a lifetime *Teacher Prep* Access Code.

CONTENTS

Mary Beattie is an associate professor in the Department of Curriculum, Teaching and Learning at the Ontario Institute for Studies in Education (OISE) at the University of Toronto. Professor Beattie's teaching and research interests are grounded in teachers' professional knowledge, narrative inquiry, and holistic education. She teaches in the graduate and teacher education programs at OISE and also has extensive experience in K–12 classrooms. She has taught in Canada, the United States, the United Kingdom, and Ireland, and she has given keynote addresses at conferences and workshops around the world.

Professor Beattie has published articles, book chapters, and books. Her most recent book, *Narratives-in-the-Making: Teaching and Learning at Corktown Community High School,* was published by the University of Toronto Press in 2004. *The Art of Learning to Teach: Preservice Teacher Narratives* was published by Prentice Hall in 2001. *The Construction of Professional Knowledge in Teaching: A Narrative of Change and Development* was published by Teachers College Press in 1995.

Her passions and preoccupations include music, literature, nature, walking, and people with a sense of humor.

Letter from One Teacher to Another

> *When you make sense of something, it tends to disappear. It is only mystery which keeps things alive. . . . Things only disappear, only become lost, because you've stopped thinking about them, stopped living with them in some vital way. Things and people have to be planted in you, have to grow in you, and you have to keep them alive. If you forget to keep them alive, you lose them. Many people have walked out on life because they stopped seeing it. Many have fallen into the abyss because they were looking for solid ground, for certainties. Happy are those who are still, and to whom things come. Answers are like that. They go to those who expect them. So, if you want to find something find it first. . . .*
> *How?*
> *Find it in yourself, I suppose.*

> Ben Okri

DEAR PROSPECTIVE TEACHER:

Welcome to a book that is about the creation of a professional knowledge and a professional identity in teaching. I will be your guide as you engage in reflection and self-directed narrative inquiry throughout the text. As you read the narratives presented here, reflect on them, respond to them, and learn from them. In my role as guide, I will help you to see how prospective teachers like yourself transformed their thinking and their practices through self-conscious reflectiveness and inquiry. As you read, I will be there with you, pointing out the ways in which other prospective teachers have created a professional knowledge in teaching from what initially seemed to be unrelated sets of life experiences and disconnected bodies of

1

knowledge and skills. As your guide, I will be directing you to look at the ways in which these individuals gained deeper and more profound insights into the role of the teacher, to find their own voices and values, to see how their individual and collective actions could influence change, and to create new scripts for their work in classrooms and in schools. My purpose throughout is to enable you to do this in your own life. In the end I will be there with you, guiding you as you write your own narrative, as you make plans to invent the future and to enact it in your professional practices.

The prospective teachers throughout these chapters tell how they came to recognize the ways in which past experiences and the stories they had heard throughout their lives shaped their identities and the knowledge they brought to the teacher education setting. They explain how their inquiries provided frameworks for the exploration of that knowledge and for the development of knowledge of subject matter, of pedagogy, of interpersonal relationships, and of the creation of learning environments for students. Through these self-directed inquiries, they conducted action research into their own lives and attempted to make sense of how people, systems, and relationships work together in educational settings. Their accounts of professional learning describe the difficulties and complexities of articulating deeply held values and personal philosophies, of developing a tolerance for ambiguity and uncertainty, and of struggling to discover where self-interests and communal interests meet. Their narratives provide texts you can step inside and find support for your own professional inquiry. They provide support for the recognition of your own humanity and that of your students, for the acknowledgment of your strengths and weaknesses, and for working with them in the context of your personal and professional goals and purposes.

My own story of teaching and learning and my values, beliefs, and theories of teaching and learning are deeply embedded in the text. You will hear my voice as I introduce each of these narratives and follow up with questions and suggestions for you to reflect upon and to talk and write about. I will encourage you to locate your own authentic voice and urge you to describe your experiences as you know them and expand the range of your voice by listening to the perspectives of others, especially those that differ from your own. My voice is stronger and more distinctive now than it was when I was in a position similar to yours, beginning my journey in teacher education and envisioning my professional career. It has been developed through reflection and inquiry throughout my years of teaching and within relationships with students and colleagues. It has been enriched and expanded by the privilege of helping others to learn, a privilege that guides my work now just as it was central to my original motivation to be a teacher. My philosophy of teaching and learning can be heard in the choices and decisions I make throughout these chapters, just as they are evident in my classroom actions and in my professional life.

In my career so far, I have taught students in Europe and North America, students from kindergarten to graduate school, experienced teachers in the middle of their careers, and prospective teachers who are just beginning theirs. In all of these situations, I have learned something about human relations, about the person and professional I am, and about the art of teaching. One of the most important lessons I have learned is that the relationship between teacher and student is at the heart of good teaching. I have learned that good teachers are centrally concerned with the creation of authentic relationships and a classroom environment in which students can make connections between the curriculum of the classroom and the central concerns of their own lives. Good teachers help students to identify their purposes, to respect themselves and others, to show compassion and tolerance, and to develop the qualities and habits necessary for full participation in life inside the classroom and out in the community. This kind of teaching requires not only a sound knowledge of subject matter and of pedagogical strategies, but also a deep understanding of students and the ways in which they learn.

Teachers must know how to create relationships and learning environments in which students feel they are valued members who are responsible for maintaining those relationships and environments. This kind of teaching cannot be reduced to strategies, plans, techniques, or styles. It cannot be prepackaged or prescribed. Making students' learning the focus of teaching and emphasizing commitment, compassion, and the capacity for true collaboration with students in their learning provide the impetus and inspiration for lifelong professional learning, ongoing inquiry, and professional joy. It has taken me a long time to come to these understandings just as it takes a lifetime to become a good teacher. The becoming is always a work in progress, and the narrative is always a temporal one that will change in the light of new experiences and new understanding.

In my work with the individuals you will meet throughout these chapters, I have helped them to find their own authentic voices, to tell the stories of their professional learning at a certain point in time, and to document their stories so they and others can learn from them. As their accounts demonstrate, the narratives are temporal portraits, or "snapshots in time." They capture the details of learning and unlearning, of changing views and perspectives as the authors were influenced by new experiences, understandings, and worldviews over time. The narratives show how prospective teachers learned new ways of knowing and of being more awake to the realities and lives of the people they taught.

As individuals, we accept science as the story of the way things are in the natural world and history as the story of past events. We also acknowledge that these stories change when new knowledge and insights are brought to bear upon them or new paradigms are discovered.

Likewise, we accept the stories, the knowledge, the ideas, and world-views we have inherited in our lives until new knowledge, ideas, and worldviews cause us to revise our understandings and the stories of ourselves that we tell and enact. When we ask such questions as "Whose history is this?" "Whose definition is this?" or "Whose version of reality is represented here?" we embark on an inquiry that can cause us to review what we thought were certainties. Change can result from this kind of questioning of the status quo, and from reflection and inquiry when we acknowledge that our knowledge is partial and that it can be expanded through hearing the perspectives of others. We accept that inquiry is a never-ending process and that we must be willing to be lifelong learners.

As you embark on this professional learning journey, it is important to acknowledge that you have many significant experiences in life and in formal education settings from which you can now learn. You probably have in excess of 20 years of experience in formal education settings where you have developed understandings of what it means to teach and to learn. You have also learned many valuable lessons in the school of life and have well-established (though probably implicit) theories about teaching and learning. You will find that all of these experiences are rich sources for reflection, discussion, conversations with professional colleagues, and reflective writing. As you uncover your memories of schooling and make explicit your understandings of teaching and learning, you will find that much of what you know has been learned from the perspective of a student where you were focused primarily on your own learning. Now as a prospective teacher, your focus and responsibility must be on the learning of all students, many of whom come from different cultural and social backgrounds to yours, and who learn in ways that are very different from the way you learn.

As you explore the memories of your own schooling, remember that much of what your teachers did and thought was hidden from your view. As a student you did not have access to the array of choices available to the teacher or the decisions made in the preparation for any given class. As a student, you probably did not know the teacher's philosophy of teaching and learning, aspirations for teaching, or the ways in which that individual understood and assessed success in teaching. Now, as a prospective teacher, you will need to explore the knowledge of teaching you have gained from your prior experience and to recognize the partiality of that knowledge. You will expand your personal understanding by drawing on current theory, new experiences in schools, and conversations with colleagues and students. In doing so, you will bring your personal knowledge to the surface, make it explicit, and reconstruct it in the context of creating a professional knowledge in which the personal and the professional are fused.

As a beginning teacher you will need to be patient with yourself, to recognize and articulate the progress you are making, and to give yourself credit for what you know and can do. You will need to be confident enough to question and challenge some of what you know and to be open to learning from and with others. At the outset, you should establish ways to document your thinking, your practices, and your questioning. Your reflective writing will provide you with a way to do this, and to track your growing capacities to connect theory and practice as they interact in your life. You must develop ways to really listen to students' voices and to hear them in their own terms, to observe them, to enter their realities, and to see the world from their perspectives. Your students will teach you if you listen to their stories, if you ask them what is going on in their lives and how it can be understood. They will teach you how to create respectful, trusting, and empathetic relationships with them and provide you with ways in which to support their learning. This kind of teaching requires flexibility and adaptability, an attitude of openness, and the willingness and capacity to learn from and with students, colleagues, parents, and others. It requires attentiveness to the persons with whom you are interacting and to the qualities and nuances of their responses. To teach in this way on a daily basis requires commitment, creativity, and imagination. When the celebrated Canadian violin teacher Lorand Fenyves (1998) was asked to explain the secret of his success as a teacher, he said, "You must be able to transform yourself to deal with students. You have to enter your students' heads and think like them. Even when you are instructing young children, there must be an understanding based on mutual respect" (p. C8).

The authors of these narratives acknowledge that at the outset their teaching practices and the stories they were enacting in their lives were largely unexamined, taken for granted, and accepted as the way things are. As you read their narratives, you will be reminded of the extent to which we all forget that the worldviews, stories, and practices we enact are cultural constructions that have become part of the fabric of our everyday lives. When we travel to other countries, we see how other societies and cultures enact different practices, conventions, and worldviews. It is often a surprise to find that our views, our attitudes, and our stories are not universally shared. Through the processes of inquiry, these beginning teachers show how they came to understand that some "official stories" and accepted norms of the cultures and communities in which they had lived were restricting and confining for them in their roles as teachers in a multicultural, multilingual, and democratic society. In their efforts to be more responsive and ethical to others, they faced up to what they saw and heard, and learned to name, resist, and take action against limiting behaviors, structures, and constructions of reality. They learned to imagine how things could be otherwise and to rescript the stories of teacher-student relationships, to make classrooms and schools collaborative learning communities, and to enact these stories of positive change. The novelist James Baldwin wrote, "Not everything that is faced can be changed, but nothing can be changed until it is faced." As you read and respond to these narratives, I hope you will be encouraged to face up to the experiences and the stories that have shaped your life, to explore the ways in which they influence what you say and do, to identify the range of possible choices available to you, and to imagine, rescript, and enact new narratives.

As your guide in this self-directed inquiry, I hope the narratives you read here will offer inspiration and support for your inquiry and provide frameworks in which you can rehearse the future scripts of your career. I hope they will stimulate you to ask how you can relate to students and colleagues in new ways, and inspire you to act collaboratively to bring about positive changes in the classrooms, schools, and communities in which you work. Wherever we are in our teaching careers, we all need stories to stimulate our imaginations and actions, to support our ongoing reflections and the continuous rescripting of our future lives. Carolyn Heilbrun (1988) explains the importance of these stories to our professional lives:

> *What matters is that lives do not serve as models; only stories do that. And it is a hard thing to make up stories to live by. We can only retell and live by the stories we have read or heard. We live our lives through texts. They may be read, or chanted, or experienced electronically, or come to us, like the murmurings of our mothers, telling us what conventions demand. Whatever their form or medium, these stories have formed us all; they are what we must use to make new fictions, new narratives. (p. 37)*

These narratives are intended to inspire you and stimulate your inquiry into the creation of a professional knowledge that is uniquely yours.

- May you find personal meaning and fulfillment in your teaching career ahead.
- May the good you do for others be returned to you a hundredfold.
- May you use your special gifts to leave the world a little better than you found it.

All the best,
Mary Beattie

CHAPTER 1

Beginning the Inquiry: Documenting the Journey of Professional Learning

It has been said that if we as individuals are to determine what our relationship is to some idea of the good, "we must inescapably understand our lives in narrative form, as a 'quest.'"

C. TAYLOR

Doug Kirkaldy's account of professional learning shows how this prospective teacher acknowledges that teaching and learning are not accomplished by disembodied intellects but by people whose minds are connected to their bodies, their feelings, their hearts, and their spirits. He is willing to acknowledge what he sees and hears without an attitude of defensiveness, and to deal with the surprises, ambiguities, and uncertainties of professional learning with honesty and courage. Doug responds with compassion and caring to the life situations that interfere with students' learning in the classroom, and he accepts the necessity to do some unlearning of his past views and teaching practices. By working around the situations and obstacles that get in the way of students' learning, Doug reveals himself as a teacher who respects their humanity, their perspectives, their learning, and their lives. His story illustrates the value of authentic relationships with students and the open communication that can take place within those relationships as sources of professional learning. It shows how this prospective teacher is becoming aware of the social realities that provide a context for his work. His narrative illustrates his burgeoning understandings of the human issues that affect his classroom practices, and his growing abilities to manage the dilemmas of daily classroom life.

DOCUMENTING THE JOURNEY OF PROFESSIONAL LEARNING

> *If I have the belief that I can do it, I shall surely acquire the capacity to do it even if I may not have it at the beginning.*
>
> Mahatma Gandhi

Create a Professional Portfolio of Writing

Create a portfolio of writing that documents the details of your reflections and inquiry as you engage in the reading, writing, discussions, and conversations presented throughout this text. Tell the stories of your learning experiences, of your unlearning experiences, of your reflections, arguments, frustrations, struggles, questions, connections, and joys. Your portfolio will be a place to keep all your reflective writing as you document your learning journey by creating a trail of your thinking, meaning making, and professional learning over time. Put a date on everything you write. Write in your own authentic voice, and write for your own purposes. Keep your "inner critic" at bay as you write, and remember that it will be your decision regarding which pieces of writing you will make public and which you will keep private. All of the first-draft writing you do will no doubt be private, but it will provide a repository for your ideas and your thinking, and become a basis for future drafts and for the narrative you will write.

The ongoing reflective writing you do will help you to articulate what you are learning, build self-knowledge, and understand how this is contributing to your growth as a teacher. When you read back over the details of this writing, they will provide you with valuable insights into the ways in which you have made meanings and understandings, related issues and ideas to your professional practice, and imagined alternatives. This writing will be the resource you will draw on when you weave the threads of your personal and professional life into a coherent whole in your narrative. You will be able to use the narratives written by prospective teachers throughout the text and the questions following them to stimulate ideas and issues for you to reflect on, discuss and respond to, and stimulate your own reflections and writing. The activities following each narrative will help you to locate the central values and purposes at the heart of your desire to become a teacher, articulate your personal philosophy of teaching and learning, understand and enrich your classroom practices, and plan your future professional growth.

The narratives you will read throughout these chapters were written by prospective teachers who were enrolled in a teacher education program involving course work and practice teaching sessions in classrooms, throughout one academic year. During this year, these individuals created a large body of reflective writing where they documented their inquiries into their thinking, their practices, and their learning. All this writing was collected in a professional portfolio along with a variety of visuals, sketches, professional documents, artifacts, and assessments of practice teaching. The portfolios ranged in appearance, shape, and size, and they included three-ring binders, cardboard boxes, and a variety of containers deemed suitable for the purpose. The materials collected were used to explore the meaning of past experiences in the context of becoming a teacher and learning to teach, and to plan future learning experiences and actions. They were used to keep an ongoing record of questions, insights, conversations, critical incidents, reflections, responses to theoretical articles, descriptions of practices, ideas for future practice, assessments of teaching, and plans for future professional development.

The following narrative account, "What Do I Have to Do to Be a Teacher?" by Doug Kirkaldy, provides an example of one prospective teacher's attempts to make sense of his experiences in practice teaching and to begin to document his reflections and professional learning. Doug shows how he is developing self-awareness, self-observation, and awareness of his actions in the classroom. He is grappling with the big question, What does it mean for *me* to be a teacher?

WHAT DO I HAVE TO DO TO BE A TEACHER?

by Doug Kirkaldy

I was in a classroom supervising some work when a student called me over. I guess she was about 17.

She said to me, "I'd like to be a teacher. What do I have to do?"

I started with the usual, "Get your B.A. Get some experience."

"I really want to teach elementary school," she said.

"Well," I said, "have you had any experience working with young kids?"

"I work with my 2-year-old twins every day," she said.

Welcome to the new reality, I tell myself. These are not the same naive kids we were. This girl picked up her daughters at the in-house day care center two doors down the hall from her homeroom. Most of the parents with children at the center are students. The parking lot for students' cars is three times the size of the lot for teachers and other staff. Some of these kids have their own Internet accounts. They've got CDs, CD-ROMs, and CNN. And these are the kids I want to teach.

Rule number one   Don't even think of trying to teach high school the way I was taught high school. Textbooks. Jesuits. Long pointers (not just for pointing things out). These kids are worldly. They live at a much faster pace. At some schools, the periods run for 85 minutes. There's no way a bunch of teenagers is going to sit and listen to me prattle on for almost an hour and a half.

I've been out on two 3-week teaching assignments. Already I've realized my lessons have to change. They have to be alive. They have to include all sorts of activities. The information must come from many sources. Overheads, videos, handouts, and textbooks are just the beginning. People have to get up from their desks. Form into groups. I need to pass out worksheets and have materials at the ready. We need a short in-class break, but I can't let them go out into the halls. Half of them won't come back. What to do with the girl who's half asleep? The classroom teacher says she has to work, because she needs the money. She puts in a 28-hour workweek outside the classroom. I'd be half-asleep, too. Still she manages to get her assignments in. Talk to her. Stay in touch. She's a good kid. But try to avoid the so-called halo effect. In other words, don't give her a few extra marks on her essays because after all she's working so hard, not like Johnny over there who doesn't have to work and disrupts the class.

Whew.

And the material. I heard years ago that books were often out-of-date by the time they were printed. These days, information is almost out-of-date by the time it reaches the computer monitor.

When I was in high school, it seemed the teacher knew it all. These days, no one can even pretend to know it all.

Centuries ago, the monks and others had knowledge and information. They parceled it out carefully. It was a way of holding onto power. These days, anyone with a mouse and a computer has access to unlimited information. The role of the teacher—my role—has changed. I'm no longer the sole deliverer of information. I may not even be the principal deliverer of information. In my classroom, some students brought in information they picked off the computer the night before. Great. But now, we're checking sources. Where did the information come from? Why put it on the Internet? Is it accurate? I'm taking my knowledge and using it in different ways. They can get at least as much information as I can. I've become their catalyst, their interpreter. I'm helping to focus their thinking, teaching them discernment. This is all quite a stretch from "Read the rest of chapter 10 and then do questions 1 and 2 on page 165."

And I've learned something about trust. When I'm preparing my lessons, I know what answers I need to get from A to B. It's somewhat humbling, but as often as not, my answers are pedestrian. In more than a few cases, their answers have been inspiring. I've learned to trust my students. More to the point, I've learned to trust myself to trust my students. I've already gained a little more self-confidence. If the discussion takes off, set aside the lesson plan. Run with it.

And I've learned something else that every good teacher already knows. You have to love the kids. I think every professor in the program has said this to us. I've found that it's true. I relate their stories to my friends after my practice teaching. It's not enough to love Keats and Byron or the theories of communism in the pre-Gorbachev Soviet Union.

This all has been a revelation to me, even though I've done some teaching in my other life. I love teaching, and I would've taught to an empty room. I have a few friends who teach at the university level, and they love what they teach. But they don't love their students. And neither did I. That may have been good enough then, but it's not good enough now.

I sat beside a few of my students during a double-header basketball game. I talked with a few of them after class about whether Doug Gilmour would ever come back from Switzerland and play hockey with the Toronto Maple Leafs. Tiny things. But their response in class the next day was mightily changed—for the better. And I felt that my attitude toward them was friendlier, warmer, more personal.

Have I learned anything else?

Well, yes.

In my previous life, we were all adults. There were lots of put-downs and lots of sarcasm. If you couldn't take it, you probably couldn't measure up. A lot of pointing out of mistakes. Not a lot of pats on the backs. It sometimes got nasty. We were in unequal relationships, and teaching is an unequal relationship. I still remember some rebukes I received from high school teachers. I thought I'd forgotten them until this year.

In my teaching assignments this year, I've noticed the power of positive reinforcement. Students who don't usually say much literally glowed when I called on them for an answer and they got it right, and I told the whole class they got it right and thanked them for it. I had learned something about reinforcement in my university class where the professor taught us by using a very dramatic example. Two student volunteers were asked to leave the room while the professor talked to us about the three kinds of reinforcement—positive, neutral, and negative. Then we participated in an experiment. The students would come in, one at a time. They would have a task to do. They would be required to walk to the front of the class, pick up the professor's jacket, which was draped on the back of a chair, and put it on. They'd cross the room and pick up a pen from a student's desk. They would then go back to the front of the class and put the pen inside the professor's briefcase, which was closed. Finally, they would carry the briefcase across the room and put it on the overhead projector.

The first volunteer would receive only positive and neutral reinforcement. If he did something right, took a step in the right direction, the professor would praise him. If he turned the wrong way, there would be silence. Volunteer A performed the entire exercise in 2 minutes and 40 seconds.

Volunteer B was to receive only neutral and negative reinforcement. If he were to pick up the professor's jacket, nothing was said. If he walked past the jacket, he was shouted at, called stupid, and so forth. After more than 5 minutes, volunteer B had managed to put on the professor's jacket. That was all. He was frozen to a spot. He couldn't or wouldn't move. And there was an uncomfortable silence in the room.

That demonstration will stay with me for years. It was with me every day of my practice teaching sessions in classrooms. I had a little more patience on my second session. I was a little more encouraging. And I noticed a few of the kids who hadn't said a word in class before were now daring to speak out. My associate teacher noticed, too!

Should I ever return to my previous career of journalism and broadcasting, my colleagues there will also notice a kinder and gentler Doug. Especially one person who worked for me. He got from me neutral and negative reinforcement—with predictable results. That will change in my interactions with people after what I have learned.

And there are a lot of other smaller things. Like tests. I used to lecture part-time at a university in the journalism program. I spent a lot of time trying to teach the importance of teamwork. No one can be a lone wolf. The assignment desk has to help the reporter who has to keep the desk informed about her story so the lineup editor knows where to place the story and so on. Yet, every week, I'd give them a news quiz. Ten questions. Who said what this week in the House of Commons? What's Canada's predicted deficit? What's the capital of the Yukon? I was trying to teach one thing and testing and handing out marks for something else. I now realize this was not very smart.

When I arrived in the high school for my practice teaching session, the class was just wrapping up a series on democracy. The teacher had been using a traditional lecture/test approach. Can you teach democracy that way? And how far would I go? Would I let the kids decide democratically which areas of democracy they'll study? Would I let them vote on whether to have a test? If yes, how should it be constructed and assessed? What other methods of assessment could be used? I'll have to get back to you on that one.

And another small thing. I'm thinking about what I say and how I say it and recalling that in my last practice teaching, I used the word *swell*. I was teaching a few lessons on imperialism. It's not a word I use a lot, but I heard myself, two or three times in 2 days, say the imperialist forces weren't that happy with things as they were so they sent in their armies, and soon after, they found everything was just swell. And after the Revolution, the Americans didn't have to send any more taxes to Britain, and they thought that was just swell.

At the end of the lessons, I drew up a test using essay questions. Just guess which word turned up in far too many essays? They probably used the *swell* word as seldom as I did. Now, you might say, what's the big deal? And you're right. *Swell* isn't that big a deal. But if they pick up on that word, what else are they picking up? If the kids pick up on an innocuous word, imagine what they could do with biases and prejudices. I took another look at some of my notes, and I made a few changes.

leadership as well

I've been told that sometimes we teach the way we were taught, and that includes becoming our worst teachers as well as our best ones. I've realized that it's more than that. We teach the way we are. The teaching we got is a part of who we are. We have to decide what kind of teacher we want to be.

I came into the teacher education program to stretch myself.

To challenge myself.

To try something new.

To learn.

To change.

I've done a lot of that. And I'll do more.

The best measure of how I've changed will come from my students' learning.

Doug's story highlights the importance of learning from experience—one's own and that of others—and of continually adapting what is known in the light of what is being learned. It illustrates the value of opening our minds and hearts to new perspectives—especially those of students—and shows that there is much to be learned from points of view that are different from our own. Doug shows that he is willing to reflect on what he sees, hears, and experiences in the classroom, to face up to it, and to reconfigure his understandings of the teacher-student relationship, his own role as a teacher, and his classroom practices. He admits his astonishment that the realities of students' lives and of schools are very different than he expected them to be, and acknowledges that his students have experiences and lives very different from his own. He acknowledges that he cannot expect to teach as he was taught (or as he taught in his previous teaching situation) in the light of these realities. Rather than turning these surprises into difficulties, he recognizes the value of hearing students' perspectives, of exploring the logic in their points of view, and of adapting his practices and ways of responding in the service of students' learning.

DOCUMENTING THE JOURNEY: BECOMING SELF-AWARE AND MINDFUL OF PRACTICES

Until we can understand the assumptions in which we are drenched, we cannot know ourselves.

Adrienne Rich

- Using Doug's narrative as a guide, make a plan for uncovering your assumptions about teaching and learning and for developing self-awareness and self-observation in the classroom. Describe how you will look for evidence of growth in these areas.

- Write about a significant *learning* experience you have had in your life. Recall the details of the experience—the setting, the time of year, the people present, the feelings you had at the time, the lessons that have stayed with you. Describe them in writing, using as much detail as possible. Read over what you have written and consider what it tells you about yourself as a learner. What does it tell you about yourself as a teacher?
- Write about the most significant *teaching* experience you have had. As in the previous learning experience that you wrote about, describe this teaching event or moment in detail. Read over what you have written, and identify what it tells you about yourself as a teacher. Describe the ways in which you can use what you know to become the teacher you want to be.
- Write about your best and worst experiences as a student in school. Include as much detail as you can.
- Write a letter to yourself as a young child from your current situation as a prospective teacher. Explain to your younger self why you want to be a teacher, anticipate how this former self would react, and include your responses to those issues as you write.
- Write letters to your former teachers: the best, the worst, the ones who inspired you, and the ones who scared you. Tell them what you felt and thought and learned (or did not learn) as a student in their classes. Tell them how they have influenced your current teaching practice and what you have learned about teaching from them.
- Write about your favorite teacher when you were an elementary school student, a high school student, and a university student. Describe the aspects of these individual teachers that appealed to you and the teaching strategies that helped you to learn.
- Write an assessment of your current teaching practice, and define the ways in which you would like to improve that practice. Describe the attitudes, skills, and knowledge you need to acquire to become the teacher you want to be.
- Write a job advertisement for the teaching job of your dreams. Write your application letter.
- Write the speech you will give at your retirement party at the end of your career.

CONVERSATIONS WITH OTHERS

- Talk to the students you teach about their personal interests and hobbies outside school. Document the conversations. What surprises you about what they say? Describe the surprises.

- Ask students what matters most to them in life, what they want to know about, how they learn best, and what conditions make it easy for them to learn. Document the conversations. How will you adapt your teaching practices because of what students tell you about themselves and about how they learn? Write about this.
- Find out about students' lives, what they fear, hope for, and dream about. Keep track of what they say, and write about the implications for your future teaching practices.
- Write a letter to the student who has taught you the most about teaching. Describe the lessons you learned, and the way these lessons have influenced your practice.
- Write to your associate teacher in response to his or her assessment of your teaching practice. Explain how you plan to learn what you need to know and wish to be able to do.
- Ask your students about the teachers they like most. Find out what qualities they think are the most important in a teacher. Relate what they say to your own teaching practices.
- Write about a time when you were able to see the world (or one aspect of the world) from someone else's viewpoint. Explain the circumstances by which you were able to "step into another's shoes." Discuss the value of this ability in the process of becoming a teacher.

CONVERSATIONS WITH SIGNIFICANT TEXTS

- List the significant books in your life. Choose the three most significant ones, and write about how each one has influenced your life, your teaching practice, and the way you enact yourself in the world.
- Write your personal response to a theoretical article or book, a policy document, or curriculum document.
- Describe a theory of teaching or learning you find useful in your practice. Explain its usefulness and its limitations.
- Identify two professional texts or articles that have influenced or inspired you. Write about your response to the ideas presented in each of these. Describe the ways in which you believe they influence your philosophy of education and/or professional practice.
- Locate the three or four children's books that you can remember most vividly. Reread them now as an adult, recalling their significance to you when you were a child and the lessons they hold for you as a prospective teacher.
- Share your thinking and writing with others. Discuss the ideas exchanged in the context of becoming a teacher and of your personal journey in professional learning.

RECEIVING WRITTEN RESPONSES FROM OTHERS

- Assemble a collection of objects and artifacts that have particular significance for you as a teacher and learner. This collection can include music, pictures, mementos, photographs, personal documents, books, souvenirs, jewelry, toys, and items of clothing that have special and lasting meaning for you. Present your collection of treasures to a colleague or group of colleagues, explaining the meaning and significance of each item to you in the context of becoming a teacher. Ask your colleagues in advance to make notes on their observations as you speak, to identify the parts of the presentation that resonate for them, and to make note of any themes or patterns they hear in the ideas and issues presented.
- Write about the experience of making this presentation. Explore the details for insights and wisdom regarding your role and purpose as a teacher.
- Collect questions from recent interviews conducted in the school district in which you hope to be hired. With a partner, identify five or six potential questions for a job interview. Take turns to be the interviewer and the interviewee and to role-play the job interview. As the interviewer, be observant to what the interviewee says and the ways in which things are said. Take note of the oral language, body language, content, and tone of the answers, and make your notes immediately after the interview. Provide your partner with oral and written feedback on the interview.
- Imagine a school setting that nourishes the whole person of the teacher and the learner—a place where teachers' and students' minds, hearts, emotions, and spirits are engaged in the acts of teaching and learning. Imagine you are the principal of this school and you are hiring a new teacher. Design a series of interview questions you will use. With a partner, take turns as the interviewer and the interviewee. Provide your partner with oral and written feedback on the interview. Document your reflections on the experience.

REFLECTING ON EXPERIENCE, INTERPRETATION, AND MEANING MAKING

- As you document the journey of your professional learning in your portfolio, take the opportunity to reread your writing from time to time and to reflect on the meanings and interpretations you find there. Write about your reflections.

- Keep a copy of the National Council for Accreditation of Teacher Education Standards (NCATE Standards) in your portfolio. Create a separate page for each standard, and as you complete an activity that addresses that standard, make a note of the activity. Review these pages from time to time, and reflect on your growing professional knowledge, skills, and attitudes in relation to the creation of a professional identity that is true to who you are, the creation of relationships with students and colleagues, and the creation of a new script for classrooms, schools, and society.
- Reread your writing on a regular basis to explore the ways in which you are opening up a dialogue between your history and your present, in order to create new insights and understandings. Keep track of these by writing about them.
- Use the Circle of Inquiry to describe your experiences—past and present—to reflect on them, interpret and make meaning from them, and to use your new understandings to plan future actions and professional practices.

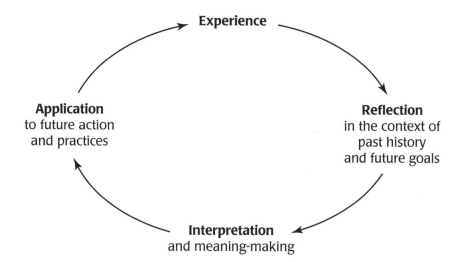

Creating a Professional Identity: Connecting the Personal and the Professional

Thinking is Easy
Acting is Difficult
And to Put One's
Thoughts into Actions
Is the Most
Difficult Thing.

GOETHE

The creation of an authentic professional identity is the major focus of the chapters in this part of the book. This process requires you to go deep into yourself, to find the central values and beliefs that sustain you in your personal life, and to connect them to your professional purposes and practices. The process is concerned with enabling you to find your voice, to link self-knowledge and professional knowledge, and to connect all the aspects of your person—your personality, passions, eccentricities and preoccupations, intellect, emotions, and moral purpose—to the processes of becoming a teacher and of learning to teach.

A holistic and narrative orientation to teacher education acknowledges the connectedness of the learner's prior experiences, current purposes, and future goals. It locates the learner at the heart of the meaning-making process and recognizes the interrelatedness of the intellectual, emotional, social, moral, and aesthetic dimensions of the individual who is becoming a teacher. This orientation to professional learning has a high degree of autonomy, self-determination, authority, and personal freedom associated

Aesthetically   Intellectually

Physically — **Creating a Professional Identity:** Connecting the personal and the professional — Emotionally

Culturally   Socially

Spiritually

with it. It acknowledges that the creation of a professional identity takes place within the context of the familial, historical, cultural, epistemological, and gendered frameworks of the individual's life.

This view of professional learning is based in relationships. Here, the curriculum of teacher education is regarded as an interactive process that connects teacher, student, and subject matter in a relational and holistic context. The construction and reconstruction of knowledge take place within this relational context, and they are concerned with the making of connections and relationships: between the personal and professional, between the teacher and the learner, between the theory and practice of teaching and learning, between the various domains of knowledge, and between teachers and their colleagues and the communities to which they belong. This orientation to teacher education challenges simplistic notions of a curriculum for professional learning based on a set of theoretical and practical requirements, a course of study, or a list of competencies. Here, the person who is becoming a teacher is deeply connected to the content of the teacher education program, the knower is intimately connected to what is known, and professional growth is understood as creating deeper connections between one's own work and the concerns of learners, schools, and society.

The narratives in this section of the book focus on the creation of a professional identity that has authenticity and coherence in the context of an individual's whole life. The knowledge and understanding these individuals bring to the teacher education setting are grounded in their personal biographies and family histories, their experiences of schooling and of growing up in different cultural and social environments, and the hopes they have for their future careers. These prospective teachers ask fundamental questions: Who am I? What do I know? What are the origins of what I know? What were the social, cultural, linguistic, and gendered circumstances in which I learned? In what ways is my knowledge partial? Who benefits from my style of teaching, and who is disadvantaged by it? What is the purpose of my teaching? What are my desired outcomes for my teaching? What are the best ways to achieve these outcomes? How can I make changes to my teaching that will enhance students' learning? What kind of teacher do I want to be? How can I become this kind of teacher? By probing beneath the surface of their intellectual and emotional responses to these questions, these individuals come to see that professional learning is different from other forms of learning in academic life. It involves far more than an emphasis on the abstract "book knowledge" of traditional disciplines and requires them to learn from a wide variety of sources, including their own past experiences. They acknowledge the involvement of the whole person in the act of learning and of knowing. They value the intellect, emotions, senses, and imagination in the processes of learning to teach, and they learn how to learn by using all the resources available. They learn to ask questions of the stories and practices they enact in their classrooms and in their lives, and to continuously plan their own growth as persons and professionals.

Each of the prospective teachers here engages in a self-directed inquiry to identify what is known; to articulate personal beliefs, values, priorities, and orientations toward teaching and learning; and to plan professional growth. Their accounts show that what must be learned is intimately connected to what is already known and to expectations for the future. They show how they learn to "think like a teacher" and describe the unique and personal ways they address the details and dynamics of learning to teach— of relating to students in the role of teacher, of dealing with classroom management issues, of presenting the subject matter of the curriculum, of assessing student work, and of creating democratic classrooms. Each narrator learns a variety of teaching strategies, explores different ways of creating safe and equitable classroom environments, and works out diverse ways of relating to large numbers of students. It is within the structures provided by these individuals' own inquiries, their purposes and goals, that they build a coherent body of professional skills and strategies and make choices among instructional methods, assessment practices, and designs for curriculum.

In chapter 2, Carol Sapiano's narrative makes significant connections between the personal and the professional and the ways in which they are deeply connected in the process of becoming a teacher. Carol's narrative addresses the following dimensions of professional learning:

- the interconnectedness of the intellectual, spiritual, emotional, social, and moral dimensions of the person who is learning to teach;
- the teacher as learner: the process of transforming personal knowledge and professional practices;
- the importance of establishing professional relationships with students;
- the power of reflective writing in enabling the teacher-learner to rethink assumptions, to connect the intuitive and the analytical, to reconstruct what is known, and to develop new practices;

- ways to connect one's central purposes and sources of satisfaction to the larger context of curriculum design and the pursuit of an ethically based professional life.

In chapter 3, Steven Hunt's narrative focuses on the centrality of personal authenticity, integrity, and self-acceptance in the creation of a professional identity. Steven's narrative addresses the following:

- the power of preconceptions and assumptions and the processes of examining, reworking, and transforming them;
- the interrelatedness of the physical, intellectual, moral, social, and aesthetic dimensions of the person who is becoming a teacher— particularly the importance of recognizing the role of the body in the professional context;
- acknowledgment of the emotional dimensions of becoming a teacher;
- the recognition of personal strengths and unique features; of belief in the self, one's own voice and ways of being in the world.

In chapter 4, Doug Stratford's narrative addresses the uncertainty and ambiguity, the mystery and the beauty at the heart of learning. It honors the creativity that is central to the learning process and the process of learning to teach. Doug's narrative deals with the following:

- the teacher as learner: learning to teach as a creative and artistic process where ambiguity, contradictions, and dilemmas abound, and where inquiry is understood as continuous improvisation and creation of meaning;
- recognition and authentication of the emotional aspects of becoming a teacher: dealing with self-doubt, personal shyness, and lack of self-confidence in the context of professional learning;
- learning to teach by identifying one's own purposes and aspirations as a teacher and by connecting them to curricular content and to students' interests and personal agendas.

In chapter 5, Wendy Barber's narrative considers the value of learning from past experience in the context of becoming a teacher. Wendy's chapter addresses these issues:

- learning from one's own past experiences—personal strife and painful experiences as rich sources for professional learning;
- self-acceptance, self-worth, and self-respect as integral aspects of a personal and professional identity;
- acknowledgment of personal strengths and gifts and of using them to create relationships with students and to develop as a teacher;
- understanding teaching as a relational activity: becoming a caring, empathetic teacher, which encompasses care for the self and care for students.

CHAPTER 2

Making Room for the Aesthete: Accommodating the Self in Teaching

Students are alive, and the purpose of education is to stimulate and guide their self-development. It follows as a corollary from this premise, that teachers should be alive with living thoughts.

A. N. WHITEHEAD

Carol Sapiano's narrative shows how the personal and professional dimensions of becoming a teacher are intimately intertwined as knowledge is built through inquiry. Carol describes the creation of a professional identity that is true to the person she is and to the professional teacher she wants to become. Her narrative shows how her central values and beliefs provide a structure for her professional inquiry, enabling her to identify the various choices available to her and the ways to develop her practices. She uses increased self-knowledge to learn what she needs to know and to direct her professional development.

Carol makes extensive use of reflective writing to conduct her inquiry and to explore the significant life experiences that have shaped her understandings of teaching and learning. Through the writing, she acknowledges her personal and cultural heritage, accepts the necessity to balance tradition and innovation, and embraces her right to write the script for her present and future professional life. Through her analysis of the writing done over time, she recognizes the connections between her need to establish creative, democratic classrooms where her students will create new knowledge and understandings, and her desire for creativity in her personal life. The analysis of the writing allows her to recognize the aesthetic and emotional rewards she feels when she helps others to learn, and to use this knowledge to make decisions and to manage dilemmas. Carol's increasing self-knowledge enables her to understand her efforts to "encourage freedom of thought, speech, and action," her desire to "make space for the emergence of student voices and open windows in their minds," and to pursue these as worthy goals in her teaching.

Carol's inquiry enables her to understand her desire for student engagement in the learning process, her affinity for teacher-student relationships with equitable power and control, and her need to create a democratic classroom. It enables her to make sense of the dilemmas and frustrations she feels and to identify her purposes as a teacher. It leads her to explore the connections between her existing knowledge of teaching and learning, and her experiences as a high school student. She documents the feelings of frustration she had as a high school student and recognizes that she has no desire to replicate the relationships of power and control she experienced then, in her current teaching life. She realizes that if she is to learn to teach in ways other than how she was taught, she must resist the pressure she feels to replicate those relationships of inequitable power and control. She must reconstruct and rescript them. Carol's narrative is testimony to the faith she has in herself and in her students, and to her will to pursue what she believes is possible. It illustrates her quest to make more intimate connections to herself, to the students she teaches, and to the social and educational communities in which they live.

SOLUTION: MAKE PLANS AND BE PREPARED TO CHANGE THEM

by Carol Sapiano

Back at the deli counter, I snapped a ticket off of the big red number machine and am waiting my turn. "54?" bellows Maria, a first-generation Italian mother of three who usually proves to be the highlight of my grocery excursions. Maria is quick and efficient, and, most exciting of all, she has a hearing problem. Trust me, I have chosen my words carefully—it is exciting. How? Well, because I always know the things I need to buy at the deli counter. I'm just never sure I'll find them all there when I unwrap the brown paper packages at home. For example, today I had planned to prepare veal scaloppini, marinated asparagus, and a tossed spinach salad for my guests. Maria, however, had other plans. . . .

Unwrapping all of the neat deli packages, I found chopped prime roast in the package that was supposed to be the veal. The first time this happened 3 years ago, I think the neighbors heard my "Ahhhhhh!" from across the street. I don't usually have a car, you see, and I have a nasty habit of going menu shopping hours before the guests are scheduled to arrive at my home.

What can I say? I take risks; hence, I still eagerly anticipate my "encounters" with Maria. What to do? Guests are coming over and my plans have been ruined. . . .

Solution: Change Plans!

At first, this much-feared, impossible task was accomplished after hours of cursing and slamming things around in the kitchen because I hadn't the slightest idea what to do with whatever it was I did not order. Eventually the notion of actually picking up a cookbook rather than simply relying on past experience occurred to me. But then, this wasn't just any old cookbook. It was one filled with dishes prepared by exotic cultures of foreign lands whose recipes called for Maria's surprise ingredients. Over time (thanks to Maria) I have become a multicultural culinary artiste extraordinaire. Don't let the title confuse you, it has much more to do with the ability to adapt to new if not foreign situations and being able to measure choice ingredients, than any magic at all.

(Professional Journal, 03-12-94)

So what does all of this have to do with education, you ask? My answer is that the metaphor of the chameleon describes my process of becoming an effective teacher, and this metaphor and the others I have also used provide a portrait of me as a teacher. I have learned that being an effective teacher is much like being a chameleon. Just as the chameleon is a beast that changes color to adapt to disparate moods of panic, pleasure, or pain, so, too, must a teacher be able to adopt a multitude of personae to suit the needs of different students and situations. The practicality of being chameleon-like was most evident during the first few days of my practice teaching sessions in my teacher education year. Picture this: a room occupied by one student teacher and approximately 25 students who are already at an advantage in their experience of working together as a class, before the arrival of their "guest." If learning is to take place during their minimal time spent together, some adaptations must occur. Which is more pragmatic, having the 25 adjust their learning styles to the student teacher's teaching style, or vice versa? Think about it. . . .

For starters, each new classroom, principal, school board, and student will be a surprise. As I've grown to understand it, there doesn't seem to be much room for assumption in this "business" because things are always changing. Doing things differently or adapting to meet these changes isn't as difficult as it appears. It's just a matter of exploring these new frontiers, getting comfortable, and generating a "recipe book" of ways to handle transition, whether it's the grade nine reform, alternative lesson plans, an attitude that welcomes change, or simply a willingness to try new things.

(Professional Journal, 03-12-94)

Teacher as Zen Buddhist Yashiko

One of the greatest compliments I have ever received from students is their assertion that my presence as a teacher tends to be enigmatic. What one particular class of grade 12s discovered during my stay with them was that I was everything but what they had been conditioned to expect of an English teacher. I used Socratic strategies minimally, refused to preach my knowledge and expect them to embrace it without question. What I did was to encourage freedom of thought, speech, action, and "alternative" learning. I also made space for the emergence of student voices and opened windows in their minds. I tried to accomplish this by challenging what they accepted as truth, baiting them, tantalizing and teasing them with ideas that raised their curiosity to a point at which they had no option but to pursue them independently. I tried to "answer" their questions with other "guiding" questions so that they could learn to take responsibility for their own learning. I know that my questions sometimes frustrated them because many had grown accustomed to depending on teachers to learn for them by unconditionally providing the answers to questions instead of having them think for themselves.

> My experiences with students both in class and out of it have helped me realize that teaching, in all its grandeur, is simply about making a connection with students.
>
> Opening this channel of communication includes, above all else, listening to the emerging voices of learners as unique individual persons and validating both their experience and their self-worth. The most valuable lessons to be learned are not found in English, the sciences, math, physical education, music, languages, technology, family studies, social sciences, or religion, per se. These serve as the machinery with which to probe and explore the lessons in life that students will carry with them past graduation. Taking a stand and defending it, thinking creatively, critically, and independently, getting along with others regardless of differences, being aware of one's strengths and limitations, and respecting, caring for, and believing in oneself—these are the lessons that matter.
>
> (Professional Journal, 10-22-93)

At times, I wanted so much to give in and "solve" their problems. Then I remembered the words of wisdom from Mr. Lau, a Zen Buddhist *yashiko*, a term somewhat similar to the North American concept of a mentor. His advice to me was "Observe. . . . Think much. . . . Speak little. . . . Allow the young to grow in knowing." At the time, I wondered skeptically about how students could grow if the teacher spoke little. We discussed the concept at length, after which I came to the realization that discovery, not memorization, was fundamental to students' acquisition of knowledge because only through discovery did students actively participate in their own learning and, hence, grow in their experience.

In our conversation, Mr. Lau did not solve the problem for me. Rather, he guided me through my "confused" phase by breaking the problem down into manageable parts, encouraging me to consider each part in isolation and then the basic premises of all of the parts in the context of my original problem. From this enlightened yet humble and simple man, I learned the importance of learning to learn—the fundamental curriculum that lies beneath curriculum.

> By spending time with students outside of class I found that, to really help them to improve, I had to help them to realize that the process of improving has more to do with self-esteem and independence than it does with essay writing. My motto in these sessions was "You've got what it takes; you just haven't learned to use it yet." Rather than drawing attention to and emphasizing their weaknesses (as was done to me) this teacher believes in helping students to strengthen themselves and of using reminders of their strengths to encourage the attainment of their goals.
>
> On the last day of my first practice teaching session students approached me with a card signed by all of their classmates. In it, they weren't thanking me for the innovative lessons, creative presentations, or for the hours I had spent researching and reading to fulfill what I had perceived to be my foremost responsibilities as a teacher. Instead, they thanked me for sharing my stories, and for laughing, but most of all for pushing them, mentoring them, believing in them.
>
> (Professional Journal, 10-22-93)

Throughout my journal writings I have asked, "But how is it that students allow a teacher into their lives this way?" I found answers in the traditional Japanese relationship between mentor and student. This relationship is based solely on trust—trust that the mentor has earned and not been endowed with by virtue of his title. Simultaneous images of mentor and chameleon come to mind as there is no one prescribed method of earning the trust of students. All classes are not the same, and the mentor must observe the likes and dislikes of students, that which elicits respect and, conversely, that which denies respect. The chameleon must adapt to these observations, keeping in mind that she chose this profession for others and not for herself. This is the thinking that finally makes sense for me—the invisible agenda that took me nearly 8 months to work out. By reflecting back on my teaching experiences and my attempts to interpret these in journal writings, the colors became clearer and more vibrant. An excerpt from my journal shows how I was trying to work it out:

> The students' trust in my experience comes slowly as the result of honesty, Job's patience, demonstrated knowledge of subject matter, confidence, well-roundedness, concern for the welfare of each individual student, ability to remain cool, calm, and collected during

crises, open-mindedness, availability to students as listener, identification of self as learner, respect for students and their experience, and much much much much much much much much much much much much much much more.

(Professional Journal, 04-10-94)

The literal translation of *yashiko* from ancient Japanese is "enlightened one," which necessitates the inclusion of a spiritual dimension to this image of teacher. A further excerpt from my professional journal shows how I was learning about this in the context of my life as a teacher:

> I am a Roman Catholic whose faith is alive in all that I do. This doesn't mean that I attempt to convert every person I meet. What it does mean is that I lead my life in a way that reflects my spirituality. My faith is a very simple one, really. It has everything to do with respect for oneself and for others—a value I hope to instill in each and every one of my students, Catholic or not. My insistence on students' respect for others includes both women and men, heterosexuals and gay persons, all races, creeds, and cultures equally.

(Professional Journal, 02-13-94)

My spirituality manifests itself in the example I try to set as a role model in the classroom. I do not hesitate to use sacred texts and myths in my English class, encouraging students to explore their human values, to feel their power, and thus to draw inspiration from them. I hesitate to call myself a religious person because that would limit my spirituality to an observant participation in a specific ritual and would restrict my image of mentor to the Roman Catholic sphere. In my experience in both public and separate schools, I sensed a yearning in students for an opportunity to be able to integrate the spiritual into their lives. In a drama class I was teaching, students asked silently for guidance by choosing to enact a tableau entitled "Important Things" to the song "True Believers" by Kevin Jordan. The lyrics speak of a generation of lost adolescents who are confused about spirituality because they lack role models in a hypocritical society of "believers." The next day I responded to my grade 12s in their language of silence quoting the Koran, which I found on the compact disc sleeve of the popular new age soloist Enigma:

> I tried to find Him on the Christian cross, but He was not there; I went to the Temple of the Hindus and to the old pagodas, but I could not find a trace of Him anywhere.

> I searched on the mountains and in the valleys but neither in the heights nor in the depths was I able to find Him. I went to the Caaba in Mecca, but He was not there either.

I questioned the scholars and philosophers, but He was beyond their misunderstanding.

I then looked into my heart and it was there where He dwelled that I saw Him; He was nowhere else to be found.

> Jelaluddin Rumi (from the album *The Cross of Changes*, Enigma, Virgin Records, 1993)

Once more I failed to conform to their expectations because I didn't preach to them or attempt to indoctrinate them. I merely observed, guided, and encouraged them in the spirit of yashiko (mentorship).

Teacher as Subtle Terminator: Combining Subtlety and Creativity

Rocco decided that Ms. Sapiano was up for a test:

All had been going well up until 2:05 at which time I felt a tap on my shoulder. I had been sitting near the back of the class listening to book report presentations when I heard an all too familiar voice ask if he could go to the bathroom. I turned, trying as hard as I could to hide my irritation (since these bathroom visits had proven to be cigarette breaks and we had agreed the previous day that they would not happen again) and plainly said "no." Shocked, he gave off a sarcastic sneer and then walked out the door.

What to do? I didn't want to disturb the rather bashful presenter, but at the same time I knew I had to do something.

Everything started to move in slow motion. I got up, smiled, and nodded encouragement to the solitary girl at the front of the class, made my way over to Rocco's desk, collected his jacket, his sweater, his books, and his bag, made my way over to the door, opened it, gently put his belongings on the floor outside closed the door and locked it. I remained leaning against the door, a "just in case" precaution, and questioned the presenter from there. Midway through one of her answers, Rocco kicked the door from the outside. . . . I left the door half-open and turned to find a red-faced, raging, 18-year-old boy.

Looking him straight in the face, I calmly said, "No means no in my class, no exceptions. Not even for you."

(Professional Journal, 10-21-93)

During my practice teaching sessions, I had much cause to contemplate classroom management. I had struggled long and hard with the issues of power and control while I was a student, so I was naturally committed to avoiding the mistakes my teachers had made. I learned about dealing with different levels of discipline problems and about developing a general framework from which to develop my own management strategies. The theory of the "bump sequence," which I had been taught, did not work for me because it was not my own, and hence it clashed with my general approach to teacher-student relations. Rather than wait for problems to arise to deal with them, I much prefer to set them straight from the beginning.

I only have one rule in class; it has three parts, but nonetheless it remains one rule. I do not ask or request but *require* respect for peers, the learning environment, and the teacher. In advance, I promise to respect them in return and to earn their respect, at which point I have them sign a behavioral contract regardless of age, grade, or learning level. I polish off my little spiel with a reminder that I will not tolerate disrespect at any level, at which point I usually crack a joke of sorts to remind them that unlike the Terminator, I am human!

> Class began at precisely 1:17 the next day—a first since I had been there. Rocco made an appearance in an impeccable uniform, another first, and remained a portrait of perfection for the rest of the period. His homework was done, he took lecture notes quietly and even offered to set up the VCR. I accepted this wordless apology by making eye contact with a smile as he left the room, sheepishly wishing me a good weekend.
>
> (Professional Journal, 10-21-93)

The issue of subtlety comes into play when I am forced to put my promises into action. I do not walk into "power traps," yell, holler, curse, raise my voice, turn red in the face, beat my fists on the desk, throw things, or send students down to the principal's office. These are a waste of my time and my energy. I do, however, take a few seconds to think about the fastest, most democratic, and cleanest way to terminate the disruption and move on as though nothing happened. I rarely lose control, nor do I allow students to even think about trying to take advantage of me. How? I keep them too busy to do anything but stay on task. Also, and importantly, I try to be personable. Students tend to think twice about "messing" with a teacher they actually like. There are always dangerous issues of pride to deal with, but Rocco and others like him taught me that a mix of subtlety and creativity usually works.

Teacher as Aesthete

I take risks when I bring my aesthetic self into the classroom. . . .

One thing I've definitely learned about myself is that I'm not like any other English teacher—I'm myself. I tried denying my creativity for a very long time in my attempts to come to grips with my own identity as a person who is also a teacher. Earlier on in the school year I wrote:

> I am a dedicated musician fascinated by all types of music and willing to learn about the "noise" of the younger generations. Despite the fact that both of my subjects couldn't be farther away from music, a spinning

compact disc player can always be found in Ms. S.'s English or Family Studies classes. I dare to be different because I strongly believe that, if used strategically, music works like glue in that it bonds teacher and students closer together. Not only does it set the stage for a relaxed environment, but, if one allows the students to supply the compact discs, it also encourages the free expression of adolescent culture.

(Professional Journal, 03-12-94)

In musicians' terms, "I denied my own music and, thus, denied my own person." I am personally and professionally an aesthete because I have an appreciation for beauty, especially that which exists in art forms. I rejected this essential part of myself in the pursuit of the professional and found that this robbed me of the energy and vitality necessary for professional growth. Having discovered this, I now see that my approach to English is artistically eclectic. I integrate visual art, music, dance, and drama into the curriculum to bring it alive in its appeal to the senses. I've never understood why such strategies are restricted to art and drama classes. I intentionally break these unspoken rules and it feels amazing because it has the intended effect. It inspires. One of the English teachers who visited me said:

Carol's use of music in the classroom to tap sensory levels in the students was effective. She wrote with the students, and her jottings suggest that Carol has the beginnings of a powerful strategy to move into creative writing.

During that class, I had used flamenco music to stimulate students' creativity. I wrote, too, and shared my responses to the music with my students. I have included that response to the music of the Gypsy Kings here.

Response to the Music of the Gypsy Kings

A single guitar strums
Sonorously
In the comfortable darkness
Of the tavern as
Glasses of wine clink
Sharply
His eyes droop
Lazily

As she twirls and swirls
In Spanish costume and movement

I join her in the
Heart-beating audible embrace

We are clothed by five or six
Pairs of hands clapping
Rhythmically and slowly
As the dark green wine bottles
Sway slowly
Cupped lovingly
in their straw basket hands

(Professional Journal, 1994)

I take risks when I bring my aesthetic self into the classroom, but it is by doing so that I have found my niche. I want my students to take risks, too, and it is only when they take calculated risks and ownership that their ideas and plans become truly theirs. It is then that the magic of real learning takes place before my very eyes.

I remember when I really learned the importance of this. I was teaching piano to a number of students, and one evening I was surprised to hear the doorbell ring since I was not expecting anyone. I opened the door to find Sasha, one of my students, waiting outside. I had forgotten all about his tutorial that evening. Nevertheless, we sat down and began as though it were a regular day. As Sasha moved through a Mozart piece, overcoming all of his previous problematic areas with the grace of a professional, my own doubts faded. Sasha had come to me 2 years previously with minimal musical background and a resentment at having been forced into piano lessons by his parents. As he played before me, I felt his sense of oneness with the piece, an experience that only few aesthetes come to know in their involvement with art.

As he concluded, I stood up and applauded. He looked up at me with an expression of utter disbelief, which (as I applauded even louder) transformed into one of joy. "I never knew I could do this. . . . I've come a long way, haven't I?" he said. I had patiently guided him through the frustrations of being a new learner to the rewards of a disciplined musician. "This is what I am," I thought. "It's in me. I still have a great deal to learn, but I am a teacher."

Now I know that the chameleon, yashiko, the subtle terminator, and the aesthete are one in Ms. Sapiano, the teacher. I have also figured out a few of the things that are really important to me and that guide me in my daily life as a teacher.

Lessons to Live By

- Don't ever forget the child within who was a student once.
- Becoming a teacher is an ongoing process that requires continuous learning.
- Be aware of students' differences so that you may appreciate their uniqueness and individuality.
- Never generalize or assume anything. Ask lots of questions and listen.
- Listen, listen, and then listen some more.

- Practice what you preach.
- When in doubt, empathize.
- Regardless of how much is expected of you, remember that you are a human being and are restricted to that which is humanly possible.
- Don't rule out the possibility that you might have to change your teaching style to help a student to improve his or her learning.
- Frustration is a good thing—it serves as a reminder that you care.
- Laugh and bring laughter.
- Respect and you shall be respected.
- Believe in your students, and they will believe in themselves.
- Eat, sleep, and exercise—your career requires more than the average amount of energy.
- Helping students to help themselves is really what it's all about.
- There is more than just one way of learning. It is all right to be different.

And as my narrative unfolds:
> God grant me the serenity to accept the things I cannot change, courage to change the things I can, and the wisdom to make a difference.

 ## Reflecting, Responding, and Writing

1. Describe your responses to Carol's story of becoming a teacher. What strengths does Carol bring to her professional role? Describe them, and then identify the strengths you bring to your professional role. Describe the knowledge, skills, and attitudes that help you to be the teacher you want to be.
2. Describe the important lessons Carol has learned about learning and teaching. What images remain with you after you have read the story?
3. Carol makes extensive use of metaphor to make sense of her inquiry. What are your metaphors of learning and teaching? Describe these metaphors, make visual representations of them, present them to others, and exchange metaphors with your peers.
4. Carol's reflective writing enabled her to examine thinking, to see patterns in her life history and professional practices, and to plan her professional learning. What patterns do you see in your reflective writing that help you to understand your current inquiry?
5. Carol challenged the story of inequitable power relations that played out in her life as a high school student. She designs and enacts a new story for teacher-student relationships. Reflect

on this path, write about it, and share your writing with a colleague.

6. Carol deals with classroom management issues in the context of teacher-student relationships. She emphasizes the importance of establishing ground rules at the outset and of defining the boundaries. Identify the lessons you can learn from Carol about these issues. Discuss these with colleagues, and document your discussion.

7. Carol describes her struggle to integrate the creative and spiritual dimensions of her identity into her professional practices. What aspects of your personal identity are important for you to hold onto now that you have embarked on a course of professional learning? How do you currently work at integrating those aspects into your professional practices? Describe this in writing by documenting your efforts (even if they are not successful).

8. Describe the teacher you want to be. Identify the qualities and characteristics you want to develop and to enact in your practices. Describe your values, interests, and goals as a teacher. Work with a colleague to describe the ways you will make connections between your purposes and goals and the design of your curriculum. Be specific about your choices of instructional strategies, methods of assessment, organizational structures, choice of curriculum materials, and ways of creating the desired learning environment. Document your discussion.

CHAPTER 3

Believing in the Self: Teaching and Individual Talent

Human beings tend to regard the conventions of their own societies as natural, often sacred. One of the great steps forward in history was learning to regard others who spoke odd-sounding languages and had different smells and habits as fully human, as similar to oneself. The next step from this realization, the step which we have still not fully made, is the willingness to question and purposefully alter one's own conditions and habits, to learn to observe others.

M. C. BATESON

Steven Hunt's narrative focuses on the development of authenticity and integrity in the context of becoming a teacher. It addresses the importance of self-knowledge, knowledge of students, and continuous observation, reflection, and inquiry. Steven tells how he learned to redirect his focus from himself and own his teaching, to the students and their learning, and to acknowledge the importance of reciprocity in the teaching-learning relationship. Steven learned the value of authenticity and integrity in his own life and in the lives of his students. He learned how to make strong connections between the curriculum and the central concerns of students' lives, and to establish classroom settings that provided space for student self-expression and engagement. He learned that being an authentic teacher will involve him in a lifetime of learning, observing students, learning from them, and altering his practices to enhance their learning.

Steven's narrative highlights the humanness of the teaching enterprise and the complexities of interactions between people who all have human qualities, foibles, insecurities, comfort levels, and individual personalities. As a beginning teacher about to go out into classrooms for practice teaching sessions, he describes how his focus was trained entirely on himself.

He was concerned that his "up-to-date" appearance might be interpreted by his professional colleagues as a rejection of the traditional image of the teacher. He worried that his appearance would work against him in school settings and that his looks and lifestyle might present obstacles to his acceptance as a member of the teaching profession. Through his reflections and inquiry, he was able to confront these anxieties with courage and honesty, to overturn his preconceived ideas, and to build self-confidence. Through the inquiry he began to consider the parallel situations experienced by many students whose "coded gear," outer appearances, and personal behaviors are often misinterpreted. He recognized the need to look beneath the surface of students' appearances, the images they project in public, and the ways they present themselves to the world. He recognized the need to help students to express themselves openly, to talk about what matters most to them, and to develop self-confidence and self-knowledge.

Steven shows how one prospective teacher discovered that the focus of his teaching is students' learning and recognized that the quality of his teaching depends on the quality of their learning. He reminds us that students want to see that their teachers are real human beings with personal interests and qualities, and that they will learn from us better when we treat them as whole human beings also.

Eliminating the Attitude Barrier of "Us" and "Them"

by Steven Hunt

Dear Beginning Teacher:

As I look back over the journal I have kept during my time as a green and naive prospective teacher, I am struck by the amount of inward reflection I have done. My time in the teacher education program was a time of eye-opening experiences, and my journal writing is a record of my reflections on teaching and learning and an exploration of the kind of teacher I can be. Now that I have completed the program, I would like to share some of my thinking with you, tell you what I have learned, and offer some suggestions that may be helpful to you on your journey.

When I began the teacher education program, I was very new to the whole formal teaching experience and many of my experiences during this time were eye-openers. Most of my prior teaching experiences had come from giving educational museum tours during the summer months. My audience then was elementary students who had spent 1 hour too long in the cramped yellow bus or seniors who were more interested in where the washroom was or what kind of petunias were growing at the front entrance of the museum than in anything I tried to convey about how Amelia Earhart got off the ground to make it across the Atlantic from my tiny (but historical) home town of Harbour Grace,

Newfoundland. Nonetheless, I knew even from these rather trying experiences that it gave me joy to inform visitors about some tidbit of knowledge during their short stay at the museum. It's the personal interaction that made it all seem worthwhile—seeing the glimmer of interest in someone's eye. Although I never realized it at the time, this was where my personal philosophy of education began to develop—through these informal exchanges of conversation, through their genuine interest in what I had to share about the museum, and through my own interest in the visitor's history and background.

It's amazing to me how often that motif of genuine mutual interest came up in the writing I did about my experiences in classrooms, not to mention how well the recognition of this motif served me. I guess I've always believed that it's extremely important to illustrate to students (or to any individual, for that matter) that I—like them—have interests and live my life in ways similar to them. I also want them to realize that I am a human being with good traits and a cultural identity, but that I do make mistakes. In my view, students need to see teachers in a less dogmatic, precise, controlled way. It is time to eliminate the attitude barrier of "us" and "them." On reflection, it was always the teachers who didn't even attempt to relate to students or the ones with the attitude of "I know everything" and "you must do it this way" that populate the memories of the most uninspired teachers and my worst classes as a student. Why would that change now that I'm the one at the front of the class? (I am a nice guy, but please!) The process of alienation of teacher from student (or vice versa) is a disastrous consequence for any learning environment.

Now the question is, What do you do about it? I have come to the con-clusion that having students relate to you as an individual is half the battle, and this can be accomplished through many means. You can begin by simply telling students about the things you did on the weekend, talking about last night's sitcom or news, or even asking what's on their minds at the beginning of a class. This does wonders in terms of "breaking the ice." It gives the stu-dents a chance to see the teacher not as some distant, uncaring instructor but someone who has interests outside school life and likes to share them. I truly believe that incorporating life's experiences into the learning environment grounds it for the students in something relevant to them. And incorporating their interests and helping students to explore aspects of these in their curricu-lum allows students to become more interested in learning more. As long as a student's interest is piqued, learning becomes a pleasure, not a chore!

My main point is this: Don't be afraid to explore the possibilities of letting students know they are no less important as individuals than you are. Validating students' interests in class allows them to show their true individual-ity, and this goes a long way to fostering mutual respect between yourself and students. Furthermore, if they can feel comfortable with their individual identi-ties, it is one less issue for them to feel concerned about. In this sense I am a believer in allowing the students more means of individual self-expression without condescension. This illustrates to students that as a teacher you are prepared to give them more responsibilities as students, and, as a result, a more positive, constructive relationship between the teacher and the student will develop. This philosophy amazed me when I actually saw it in action.

During my very first classroom experience as a prospective teacher, my associate teacher never belittled any student's outward appearance or inward perspective. That same attitude was reciprocated toward the teacher, and the result of their mutual respect for one another was inspiring and progressive. It was an atmosphere where tolerance, learning, and motivation all coexisted at an astonishing level, due in large part, I believe, to the breakdown of the traditional "me/them" authority model. Without belaboring the point, I was confirmed in my belief that this could work—and work very effectively. Needless to say, I was encouraged to hold onto my idea and establish the same individual-to-individual rapport with these students.

After the first couple of classes, my students found out from my associate teacher that I was a freelance music journalist on the side. This, in their eyes, was a big step up on the credibility scale for me, for it was obvious that they could see that a teacher did have a grasp on the subject matter of the Enlightenment and the rise of Stalin and interests in other areas that were significant to their individual realities. I was at first unsure whether they should know about my pop music connections, but after some thought, I believed (and hoped) it would be a positive revelation. Boy! Talk about an understatement! I was no longer an inexperienced student teacher but rather an individual who wanted to encourage learning. Perhaps I was even a type of role model, judging from some of their comments to me on my last day there. I realize there's no second guessing some experiences, but I must admit my interactive relationship with them was a gratifying and encouraging experience. But does this mean you have to be a freelance pop music journalist on the side to gain credibility with kids as a teacher? I hope not. There are enough freelancers in the world already! Then what does it mean, you might ask?

Learning to Observe Others

> He was very into the skateboarding look, along with oversized,
> baggy jeans and, of course, his skateboard attached to his underarm.

Well, first, I have learned the importance of being myself in the classroom, so I say to you now, Be yourself! You can never expect to gain the respect of students in a learning environment if you're trying to be someone you're not. Kids have personality radars! They can see right through the artifice of a false front. That generally means don't waste your time trying to look the traditional teacher "part" unless it makes you feel comfortable. But for those of us, like myself, who had anxieties about this and laughed hysterically to think of ourselves wearing traditional penny loafers and a suit, shirt, and tie, it simply means don't risk losing the respect and attention of your students by trying to be a cardboard cutout of "the perfect teacher" (not to mention the anguish of turning blue from laughter after seeing your reflection in the trophy case at school!). After all, if you're not comfortable with who you are, how can you expect them to be? All this means is that if you're past the stumbling block of feeling good about yourself as an individual, that's one less barrier toward making a genuine interactive relationship with students who are continually going through identity crises. By being yourself, you encourage the same trait in others or at least unarm any fears of a student's own identity. On one level, it can do wonders in the genuine interaction with your students, but where do you draw the line?

We all have our own thresholds, and exploring this concept in my own professional life has given me food for thought. My own personality and individuality have been influenced a great deal by popular culture as I have taken a keen interest in it and have absorbed it by cultural osmosis. In other words, my own subconscious interactions with pop culture greatly influenced who I became in the journey of forming my own identity. Now as an educator of tomorrow, I must decide how much of that I choose to expose to students as my teaching profile. This point may seem somewhat artificial at first glance, but how one portrays oneself to students has implications as to how they perceive you as a teacher and possible mentor, not to mention as another genuine human being. So should I tell them which musical artists I admire? After seriously reflecting on this for a while, I have come to the conclusion that I would find it difficult not to. I am a human with expressions, emotions, likes, and dislikes, after all. To disguise my enthusiasm for pop culture would be dishonest for me. It would be unfair to myself, and it would be misleading to students.

Now, what does this have to do with teaching? I have come to appreciate that my own individuality—including how I appear, how I dress, how I conduct myself—should not be compromised in a school environment where individuality and difference should be encouraged and celebrated. However, for a while—even after coming to this affirmation—I was bothered and anxious about how I would be perceived in the eyes of an older (perhaps more conservative) school board administrator or principal. During one practice teaching session, my mentor teacher told me, for instance, that the fact that I wear earrings and dress unconventionally might pose a problem for a given hiring committee, simply in terms of their initial reactions. However, the same teacher suggested that I not kowtow in such a situation, that I should present myself in an appropriate manner but need not compromise my individuality. Furthermore, if I am not comfortable in expressing my true identity and individuality, how can I possibly encourage the same of my students? My point here is simply to suggest that you must explore all aspects of your personality in becoming a teacher to know where your own individuality can shine in relation to your students. I want to allow students to relate to me as a teacher who is a slightly more experienced "version" of themselves. I want to foster mutual respect and relate on a genuine level to break down traditional hierarchical boundaries between "us" and "them." The following excerpt of my journal from the fall of 1992 shows one instance of this philosophy in its glory:

> Oh . . . and it would be unfair to my journal not to take note of one very quiet grade 12 student named Andrew who seldom showed up at class. He was a nontypical 17-year-old, and refreshingly so. He was very into the skateboarding look, along with oversized, baggy jeans and, of course, his skateboard attached to his underarm. And then there was his cap—a fuzzy, floppy jester's hat. It piqued my interest in his highly developed individualism even further. I found out that he in fact was a very bright student who, at least for the time being, was much more intrigued with the social reality of his suburban subculture. This was more of an eye-opening experience than I imagined. There I was, faced with a bright teenager who was temporarily unmotivated by "the system" and with whom I was empathizing! I felt a great deal of untapped potential there and I simply began to interact with him on a genuine level. I told him that I thought his hat was great, and he told me he took a lot of flack because of his unorthodox appearance. Over the span of two weeks Andrew began showing up more at class and began to open up more in class, whereas before he seemed to me enclosed in his shell. I believe (and hope) that my genuine interest in his personality (as opposed to his lack of attendance at school) began to boost his self-confidence. I feel I was a temporary mentor for him because I identified with his unique personality and got through to his inner sense of self. On my last day of teaching there, he told me he thought I was a great teacher. When he found out it was really my first time teaching, he told me, "I wouldn't have known it." Needless to say, this one kid made everything seem worthwhile.
>
> (Professional Journal, 1992)

So when you come across "Andrews" in your teaching experiences, look at them as the jewels hidden in the earth. Appearances can be deceptive, and the trick is to look beneath the surface and connect to the person. As I look back now, the overall impression of that teaching experience provided me with a microstudy of my developing understanding of myself as a teacher. The next experience was to evolve into a macrostudy, and this one was with a mentor teacher who would say "white" and I would immediately think "black."

Learning to Listen

First and foremost, be yourself!

This time the "cast" was different, and the teacher was definitely not one with whom I shared a great deal in the educational motivation department. After observing her rather detached, condescending treatment of a class of nonmotivated, economically challenged teenagers, all I could do was empathize with the kids. Although doing so terrified me, I decided to take the plunge and put my own style of teaching to the test. I knew that either it would be a disaster, or they would begin to feel more like human beings than an audience of automatons! Once again, pulling from my own experiences, beliefs, and values, I took a risk and pulled through with amazing results. While the teacher praised my "efforts," the students expressed their gratitude and their appreciation at having their individuality recognized.

In the few short days before I took over, I made a mental note to not emulate the associate teacher in dealing with the students. In my mind, I could only think, "No wonder they don't do work or stay on task. She treats them like misbehaving 10-year-olds—or rather, she treats them as if they are the sum of their tough outer shell that many of them portray." My observations seemed to suggest that while the teacher may have appeared to be smiling at them while teaching a lesson, the truth was that her smile wasn't sincere. It was patronizing. I could see it, and, more important, the kids obviously saw it. To them it was a situation where they weren't being genuinely respected for whom they really were. In their minds it was obvious they felt no obligation to give any respect in return. As I began my "personal crusade" (albeit being terrified in the process!), I truly listened to them—before class, during class, and after class. I talked to them about who I was and what my interests are and asked them questions about their reality—what do they do on weekends, what music do they listen to, what parts of town are they from, and other "small talk." I listened, and I really was interested. I tried to break down the barriers between us, and it showed to students my willingness to show respect and interest in who they are as students and as teenagers. The results were truly amazing and inspiring! Here's how I reflected in my journal just after the experience:

> Looking back on the experience, I have truly learned a lot about education and about myself. As I have continually harped on in the past about relating to students and showing a genuine interest in their individual realities, I have been extremely fortunate in this case to have been touched by the warmth and thoughtfulness of students who supposedly only have a tough outer shell. That class of grade 10 students inspired me a great deal, and judging from their written sentiments to me, I did the same for them. It was a two-way street, and that's all I can ask for as a teacher. Students need to feel important and worthwhile. They have enough turmoil to wade through as it is. And even though a student might be wearing a baseball hat backward with a pack of cigarettes rolled into a shirt sleeve, and all of the accompanying "coded gear," his outer shell has very little to do with the individual inside.

> (Professional Journal, 1992)

When it comes down to it, two situations are never alike. But you can do everything in your power to be as receptive and interactive with students as you can and to help them make the most of their situation. I guess it means helping them feel comfortable not fitting the traditional mode and being comfortable with who they are—in the way you are yourself. This all makes me think I've come full circle, so I say to you: First and foremost, be yourself! Believe in yourself, and have as much fun as possible doing it. Accept who you are, because if kids can see that you're not comfortable with who you are—both externally and internally—you're really not in any position to instill confidence in their ever-changing teenage identities.

Moreover, kids like you to be yourself. It helps to break down the obtrusive barriers that have traditionally kept students and teachers in different realms. I know that as teachers we must always be students who are constantly learning and trying new things. The moment we assume this has changed is also likely to be the moment we begin to lose touch with what it feels like to be a student and the moment we stop inspiring students. After all, students want teachers who are genuinely interesting individuals and potential mentors. It's quite a responsibility but an extremely rewarding one. Oh, and never lose your sense of humor. It comes in handy because most kids still have theirs!

Lessons to Live By

- Be true to yourself, believe in yourself, and don't compromise what you truly believe in. Faking it just isn't worth it.
- Never judge a student by her or his outward "shell," in the same way that you know not to judge a book by its cover. Each student has a wealth of personality traits that aren't always easily unearthed.
- Take the time to truly interact with students on a one-to-one basis, and let them know tidbits about your life outside school. Letting kids know that you didn't miss last night's episode of the latest cool television show does wonders for their perception of you. (Just never let this interfere with lesson 1!)
- Bring into the class and the school curriculum references to students' everyday reality. Incorporate these as much as possible. Kids learn a lot quicker if you can relate the subject matter to a familiar notion of their experience.
- Leave any idea that you are better than students at the front door.
- Remember that teaching means never stopping learning.
- Laugh a lot!

Reflecting, Responding, and Writing

1. Describe your responses to Steven's story. Explain which aspects or details of his story resonated for you. What do you learn from his narrative of professional learning?

2. Steven's story describes the difficult process of confronting preconceived notions about what it means to be a professional, what a professional teacher must look like, and what a professional teacher's interests and hobbies might be. What is your image of a professional teacher? Describe how this person looks and acts, and what his or her interests and hobbies might be. Do you know any teachers who do not fit this image? Describe them.

3. Describe your image of a "good teacher." Describe the teacher you want to be.

4. Do you feel you have to conceal any aspect(s) of yourself to "fit in" to schools as you know them? Do you have any concerns about how much of your personal self you can reveal in professional settings? Write about any concerns, anxieties, or fears that you might have.

5. Steven describes how his preconceived notions were overturned, and how he learned that his personal appearance and interests were an advantage rather than a disadvantage in school settings. Describe a time when your preconceived ideas were overturned. How did you feel? How did it affect your future actions?

6. Describe a time when you were able to shift the focus from yourself and your teaching and focus all your attention on a student's learning. Explain the details of this situation: what the learner said and did, what you said and did, what the physical surroundings were, what time of day and time of year it was, what sounds you could hear, what emotions you felt. What did you learn from this experience? How can you use this knowledge to learn about teaching? Describe in detail an experience when you learned something significant from another person—a parent or relative, a friend or colleague, a student or a child. Describe in detail an experience when you learned something significant with another person.

7. Steven contends it is very important to include all students in the work of the classroom. What strategies for inclusion do you

use in your teaching? Describe how you create a relaxed atmosphere in your classroom where students can ask questions, talk about what matters most to them, and participate openly in dialogue and conversation.

8. Steven acknowledges that students need to feel important and worthwhile. He acknowledges the teacher's role in creating a physical environment where students feel comfortable and valued. He acknowledges his role in the creation of learning experiences which enable students to build self-esteem and a view of themselves as successful learners. Organize a large-group discussion where you share ideas, strategies, and advice about how to do this in your own classrooms. Document the discussion and your plans for future action.

9. Make a plan for the ongoing development of your reflective capacities. Describe how you intend to observe and make conscious your biases and assumptions as they are enacted in your practices. Share your plan with a colleague and discuss ways to be both critical and creative as you observe your actions, challenge what you usually take for granted, and plan your professional growth.

CHAPTER 4

Synthesizing Hyacinths and Biscuits: Creating the Artist-Teacher

The important thing about art is not what it gives us, but what we become through it.

OSCAR WILDE

Doug Stratford's narrative acknowledges the uncertainties and ambiguities, the mystery and the beauty at the heart of learning and of teaching. He addresses the connections between the creative, the emotional, the practical, and the intellectual dimensions of inquiry and professional learning. Doug shows how the process of exploring his personal purposes and motivations for becoming a teacher enabled him to take charge of his learning; to deal with his self-doubts, dilemmas, and difficulties; and to find his voice as a teacher. By going deep into his personal reasons for becoming a teacher, he acknowledges his own love for the beauty of the visual world and the mysteries of the creative process. He recognizes that his motivation for wanting to teach emanates from his desire to help others to "love with their eyes" and to "come to know the mysteries at the heart of the creative process." This understanding provides him with the impetus to reconcile the ambiguities and contradictions he is experiencing, to develop his professional confidence and competence, and to create a coherent plan for his professional growth.

Doug's narrative is testimony to his extensive background as a visual artist and to his ability to provide volumes of meaning with a few well-considered brushstrokes. He describes the complexities and difficulties of his professional journey, of knowing and not knowing, and of a sense of security mingled with insecurity. He examines the ambiguities, contradictions, and confusions he encounters, and he does it with honesty and humor. He presents the reader with a series of images that provide insights into his questioning, speculating, meaning making, and knowledge building. He shows that by examining the lenses, images, and frameworks he uses to make meaning, he uncovers the details of his knowing and professional learning, and creates a map for future explorations.

Doug describes how he finds his professional voice, and his understanding of the struggle provides him with ways to help students to do likewise. His story is a moving account of the way in which a mature and talented individual learns to overcome his shyness and self-doubt, to develop self-confidence and competence, and to find purpose and fulfillment as a teacher.

Creating the Artist-Teacher

by Doug Stratford

ME, A TEACHER?
I FIND IT HARD TO BELIEVE.

"WHAT IS IMPORTANT TO ME, THE TEACHER?"
I ASKED MYSELF.
BEING ABLE TO GET UP IN FRONT OF A CLASS WITHOUT BEING NERVOUS.
FINDING A JOB.
(HOW PRACTICAL!)
COMMUNICATING THE TRUTH.

    THESE ANSWERS ARE ALL THAT CAME TO ME
    AFTER 2 HOURS OF BUILDING A THOUGHT WEB
    ON A LARGE PIECE OF PAPER ON THE FLOOR.
    IN THE PROCESS, I HAD LOOKED BACK
    OVER 8 MONTHS OF JOURNAL WRITINGS
    AND HAD REVIEWED MY ORIGINAL FEARS
    ABOUT STARTING AT THE FACULTY OF EDUCATION.

WHAT HAD I COME HERE FOR
AND WHAT DO I TAKE AWAY?
WHAT HAVE I LEARNED OVER THE YEAR?

To be less afraid
of the unknown, to have more
"real fears
and fewer
imaginary ones"

But is that all?
(Isn't that enough?)
Did I get my tuition's worth?
(curious thought)
How much confidence do you get for 2,417 bucks, anyway?
Confidence.
My famous lack of it.
How do you measure it?

It started as a kid.
Some forgotten origin.
I wanted to be an actor, or, later
a singer. A performer.
It didn't matter—
In the spotlight, that's what I wanted!
(bloody ego!)
But somehow I became scared.
Too sensitive, too nervous, too shy.
Mr. Chicken Shit.
I had to take a "public speaking for the terrified" night school course
when I was 34 years old.
Public speaking for the absolutely terrified.
"I even think you enjoyed that,"
said my teacher
after the presentation I had nervously made.
"I did," I said, to my own surprise. (I had loved it.)

Later
I volunteered as a teacher for kids.
But I needed to take sedatives
to calm myself.

THIS HABIT LASTED TOO LONG
AND WAS VERY HARD TO STOP.

I LEARNED LATER
TO TAKE A DEEP BREATH
BEFORE I STARTED TO SPEAK.
THAT HELPED.
I ALSO LEARNED
THE VALUE OF HONESTY.
YOU CAN'T DEVELOP CONFIDENCE
UNTIL YOU FACE THIS STUFF HONESTLY
AND SURVIVE. ALL YOU HAVE TO DO IS JUST SURVIVE.

DESPITE MY WEAKNESSES AND INSECURITIES
I FOUND
THAT I COULD TEACH,
BECAUSE MY ENTHUSIASM FOR
WHAT I TAUGHT
—ART—
WAS INFECTIOUS.
I SOMEHOW
MOTIVATED PEOPLE.
(THIS I FOUND HARD TO BELIEVE.)
BUT, FINALLY,
I HEARD IT ENOUGH TIMES
THAT I COULDN'T DISCOUNT IT.
　　　THEY LIKED ME—
　　　AND I LIKED THEM.
I LOVED THEIR ARTWORK.
IT WAS SO BEAUTIFUL
(SO HONEST, SO FRESH, SO ORIGINAL)
AND THEY DIDN'T EVEN KNOW THAT.
IT TOOK SOMEONE LIKE ME (A TEACHER)
TO SHOW THEM.
THEY COULD ONLY SEE THE BEAUTY OF THEIR OWN WORK

THROUGH THE EYES OF SOMEONE THEY ASSUMED TO BE MORE IMPORTANT THAN THEM.

I WANTED TO ASK THEM QUESTIONS—

THOSE SAME DEEP QUESTIONS

THAT HAD BEEN POSED TO ME

BY MY GREAT TEACHERS.

I WANTED THEM TO DEVELOP THE CONFIDENCE TO ANSWER THOSE QUESTIONS

ANY OLD WAY AT ALL.

I WANTED TO SHARE MY FACILITY

(SOMETIMES I JUST WANTED TO SHOW OFF MY SKILL
     TO AN APPRECIATIVE AUDIENCE).

HOW I LOVED WHAT THEY SHOWED ME—

A SUNSET, A TREE, A FIGURE, AN IMAGE.

A COLOR!

I LIVED IN A VISUAL WORLD.

I THOUGHT THAT NO ONE WOULD EVER UNDERSTAND THAT ABOUT ME.

I THOUGHT I WOULD NEVER MEET ANYONE LIKE ME.

(VISUALLY SENSITIVE)

MY PROBLEM WITH WORDS AND POEMS.

WHY WERE THEY SO HARD TO UNDERSTAND?

I BECAME AN ANTIWORD PERSON—RESENTFUL OF WORDS AND THEIR POWER—

(BECAUSE WORDS WERE ALWAYS MORE IMPORTANT THAN PICTURES.)

LATER, I READ ABOUT LEFT BRAIN–RIGHT BRAIN,

LINGUISTIC VERSUS VISUAL/SPATIAL INTELLIGENCE.

THEN CAME GARDNER'S THEORY OF SEVEN INTELLIGENCES.

I REALIZED THAT THERE MUST BE MORE PEOPLE LIKE ME

WHO HAD FAILED IN A SCHOOL SYSTEM

THAT CATERED TO TYPE 2, RATIONAL, LINGUISTIC LEARNERS.

(LATER I WOULD FIND THE WORDS

OF COHEN, LAMPMAN, AND VAN GOGH,

VISUAL WORDS TO IMAGINE BY,

THAT UNDERSTOOD AS I DID

AND AS I DID NOT.

THEY TAUGHT ME THAT

WE MUST SCRUTINIZE OURSELVES MERCILESSLY

AND BE TOTALLY HONEST

ABOUT OUR DOUBTS, CONTRADICTIONS,

INCONSISTENCIES, AND DILEMMAS—

TO UNDERSTAND OURSELVES AND AVOID OUR DEADLY HYPOCRISIES.)

I WANTED TO HELP OTHERS TO SEE THE THINGS I LOVED

AND THE THINGS THAT THEY LOVED.

I WANTED TO TEACH THEM TO SPEAK THE VISUAL LANGUAGE.

HOW TO LOVE

WITH THEIR EYES

INSTEAD OF THEIR TONGUES.

I WANTED THEM

TO FEEL LIKE ME

AND TO SEE LIKE ME.

PERHAPS THIS WAS MY GREAT CHALLENGE

TO TAKE THIS SORRY WRETCH . . .

THIS BROKEN MAN . . . MYSELF—

SCARED, SHATTERED, "STRANGER ON THE EARTH"—

AND BUILD HIM BACK UP INTO A REAL PERSON.

RAGS TO RICHES.

THE POOR COMMUNIST TURNED RICH CAPITALIST.

WAS THAT THE STORY I WANTED TO TELL OF MYSELF?

WAS I REALLY SO CONCERNED ABOUT THE WELFARE

OF THE WORKING CLASS

AND SOCIAL JUSTICE?

HOW HAS **THAT THEME** PLAYED ITSELF OUT

IN MY ROLE AS A TEACHER?

AM I ANY DIFFERENT THAN THE OTHERS?

DO I STILL BELIEVE THOSE THINGS,

OR AM I HERE TO GET BETTER VACATIONS

AND A DESK JOB?

"YOU HAVE THE INDIFFERENCE OF A PROSTITUTE."

THEY DON'T DO IT FOR THE MONEY. . . . THEY JUST ENJOY HAVING THAT

POWER

OVER PEOPLE.

DO TEACHERS BECOME INDIFFERENT TO THEIR STUDENTS,
CARING ONLY FOR THE POWER THEY HAVE OVER THEM?

ARE THESE MY MOTIVATIONS FOR BECOMING A TEACHER?

OR WAS IT JUST
SOMETHING TO DO (LEARN TO TEACH)
IN AN OTHERWISE DREARY LIFE?
TO PLAY WITH ONE'S OWN FATE—
LIKE A PUPPET ON A STRING.
(FIRST, WE PUSH HIM DOWN,
THEN, WE PULL HIM UP.)

FOOD
FOR "THE BLACK DOGS OF DEPRESSION."
"DON'T YOU KNOW I'M ONLY HAPPY WHEN I'M DEPRESSED,"
SAID KAREN FINLEY.

THE DARK SIDE WAS NEVER FAR AWAY.
IT SCARED ME AT FIRST.
THAT'S HOW I KNEW
I WOULD DIE LIKE EVERYONE ELSE—
BUT THE PANIC PASSED.
I WAS LEFT FEELING THE NEED
TO PASS SOMETHING ON—"THE LIGHT"—BEFORE
IT WAS TOO LATE.
THE KNOWLEDGE
OF THE MYSTERY,
OF THE FLOW.
TOO GOOD A SECRET TO KEEP TO MYSELF,
WORTH THE FIGHT AND WORTH THE WAIT,
BETTER THAN LOVE, EVEN,
I HEARD MYSELF WHISPER.

THIS MUST BE SHARED.
THE NECESSITY OF SHARING YOUR LOVE.
STUDENTS WERE EASY TO INFECT.

THEY FEED OFF MY ENERGY;
I FEED OFF THEIRS.

PERHAPS MY KNOWLEDGE WOULD MAKE A DIFFERENCE
TO SOMEONE—
WOULD HELP EVEN JUST ONE OTHER PERSON LIKE ME TO BLOOM.
THAT WOULD BE ENOUGH.
THAT WOULD MAKE IT ALL WORTHWHILE.
KNOWING THAT I COULD MAKE A DIFFERENCE
TO "FLOW" AND CONFIDENCE
AND TO THE CONSTRUCTION OF VISUAL MEANING.
BUT HOW HAD I COME ACROSS THIS KNOWLEDGE?
I WENT BACK
TO MARIO "IL MAESTRO," TO DAD,
TO ALL THOSE TEACHERS
WHO FORCED ME TO THINK
WHEN I HAD JUST WANTED TO DO
SOMETHING EASY TO HELP PASS THE TIME,
WHO, DESPITE MY LETHARGY, FORCED ME TO SEE THE PICTURES
THAT TOLD THE STORIES OF MY MANY SELVES.
WHO FORCED ME TO SEE MYSELF BEFORE I RAN AWAY
AFRAID.

SO I SEE MYSELF TEACHING
AND I SEE
THAT I MUST TEACH DIFFERENTLY
BECAUSE I AM TEACHING
BUT I AM NOT LEARNING.
I AM NOT LISTENING.
I AM NOT SPONTANEOUS AND RESPONSIVE
(AS UNPREDICTABLE AS WAYNE GRETZKY).
FAR FROM IT.
I AM DEAF.
I AM STILL TRYING TOO HARD TO TEACH.
I MUST LEARN HOW TO LISTEN
AND TO QUESTION.

DIFFICULT PROBLEMS,

SAD AND PROFOUND,

ELUSIVE, NEBULOUS ISSUES,

WITH NO "RIGHT" WAY TO DO THINGS

AND CHALLENGED PERCEPTIONS—

ON SUCH AN INSECURE GROUND

WE BEGIN.

IT IS ONLY BECAUSE OF OUR OCCASIONAL SENSE OF

HUMOR

WE SURVIVE (JUST SURVIVE).

"POETRY IS THE ACHIEVEMENT OF THE SYNTHESIS OF

HYACINTHS AND BISCUITS,"

SAID CARL SANDBURG.

THE SYNTHESIS OF TWO REMOTE IDEAS.

THIS WAS COMPLEX,

SO COMPLEX IT WAS WONDERFUL.

SO WONDERFUL IT WAS FUNNY.

SO FUNNY IT WAS REAL.

TEACHING IS PERFORMANCE

AND PERFORMANCE IS ART AND ART

IS POETRY,

THE POETRY OF SYNTHESIZING REMOTE IDEAS.

TRYING NEW IDEAS TO LEARN NEW THINGS.

LETTING GO OF WHAT YOU KNOW AND

TRYING SOMETHING NEW.

SOMETHING WILL BE SYNTHESIZED.

BUT WHAT ARE THE MEANINGS OF THESE IDEAS?

"SAD AND PROFOUND"

"REMOTE AND SYNTHESIZED"

WHY ARE WE SEARCHING FOR MEANING

IN EVERY CORNER OF OUR THOUGHTS?

TO FIND OURSELVES, OUR TRUE NATURE?

TO FIND OTHERS?

To create?
To re-create the conditions under which the self can
reconstruct itself.

As we learn
we travel from point A to point B.
We do not have a map for this journey
as we are not sure where we will go.
So we take on a guide—a teacher.
When the journey is over
we create a map
by tracing back over our footprints.
This story is one such map.
It reminds me of where I was,
it allows me to appreciate where I am,
and it permits me to reconstruct myself, to redesign myself,
for the hope-filled road to come.

So
how can I take this bunch of pennies
and turn it into a dollar?
Of all the lessons,
what have I held onto
that makes me the teacher that I am?
What have I learned?
In a subtly balanced universe,
borne of incredible forces,
I see myself as a confused and shaky
old man on his way to an insignificant end.
But if, on this route,
I have developed some sense
of what has been important to me then
I would say that, in a nutshell, it is this—

I have built some confidence in myself and
now I feel
more solid.

Reflecting, Responding, and Writing

1. What aspects of Doug's account of professional learning resonate for you? Which lines or phrases speak directly to you? What can you learn from this narrative about finding your voice as a teacher?

2. Doug recalls that when he was a child, he wanted to become an actor, a singer, or a performer of some kind, but then he became scared, nervous, and shy. Can you recall what you wanted to be when you were a child? Did you follow your childhood dream? How have you kept your childhood dreams alive? What is your "dream" for your future teaching career?

3. Doug found inspiration and support for his learning in the words of the poets Leonard Cohen and Archibald Lampman and the artist Vincent Van Gogh. From where do you draw your inspiration? Whose words inspire you to think and learn about life? What do you learn from poets and playwrights, artists and authors, singers and songwriters, theorists and researchers? Describe this in writing.

4. What fears, doubts, contradictions, inconsistencies, and hypocrisies do you experience as you prepare to become a professional teacher? Describe some or all of these and explain how you deal with them in the context of your professional learning. Discuss this topic with a colleague and collaborate to design strategies to deal with these inconsistencies in your lives.

5. Doug uncovered the meanings behind his motivation for becoming a teacher through his ongoing inquiry and reflection. When you examine your motivations for entering the teaching profession, what do you find? Describe these motivations and their origins. Explain how this knowledge helps you to make connections between your own purposes and goals, the well-being of your students, and the welfare of the community in which you live.

6. Doug acknowledges the teachers who "forced me to think when I just wanted to do something easy to help pass the time, . . . to see myself before I ran away afraid." Discuss these lines with a colleague and relate them to your own experience as a learner.

7. Document your discussion, and use your writing to explore the ways in which your knowledge of yourself as a learner can be used to help you to become the teacher you want to be.

CHAPTER 5

Learning Self-Respect and Self-Worth: Professional Learning and Personal Past Experience

Experience is not what happens to a man. It is what a man does with what happens to him.

ALDOUS HUXLEY

Wendy Barber's narrative of becoming a teacher illustrates the process of learning from past experience. Wendy shows the value of self-knowledge, self-acceptance, and an attitude of self-worth in the development of an authentic professional identity. She describes how she came to know her values and beliefs, and to acknowledge her personal qualities and strengths as a teacher. She explains how she found her purpose in helping students to know themselves, to acquire self-respect and self-worth, and to find their way in life. Her narrative is testimony to the value of reflection in professional learning and to treating all experiences as rich sources of learning—the painful and difficult along with the positive and enjoyable.

Wendy's narrative is an example of one prospective teacher's inquiry into what she learned from past, personal strife and painful experiences about the teacher she can be. Wendy describes how she drew on those life lessons to create a personal and professional self with a strong sense of purpose and desire to help others through her teaching. She recalls the devastation she experienced when she gave up active competition in swimming, her focus on the Olympic trials, and her hopes of winning a place on the Canadian national team. Her narrative account shows how she learned to create a new vision for her life, to accept the totality of her whole being, and to work with her gifts and imperfections. Through her inquiry, Wendy learns the importance of playfulness and a sense of humor in her personal life and in her teaching. She learns to feel the joy in helping others and uses this outlook to develop her abilities to be responsive to others within the teacher-student relationship.

Wendy uses her personal knowledge to develop a professional identity in which caring and empathetic relationships with students are at the core. Drawing on her existing knowledge she focuses on helping students to develop self-respect, self-esteem, and a sense of self-worth. Her goal is to enable them to "make that courageous and terrifying leap that trust in the self entails." She shows her support and empathy for students, and she demonstrates care and concern through her actions. This prospective teacher's growing self-confidence allows her to acknowledge her abilities to design curriculum, to present subject matter, assess students' work, and structure learning experiences for diverse groups of students. Wendy's narrative shows how she has established a balance in her personal and professional lives, and a way of finding meaning and purpose in her teaching.

Learning in Retrospect

by Wendy Barber

Summer 1966

I am 4 years old.

I will be starting kindergarten in the fall, and my ambitious and caring older sister has decided to teach me to read before I go. I'm not sure if this is so she won't be embarrassed by me later. (I only suspect this because, though it was her responsibility to escort me to school for that first day, she made certain that I and my kindergarten pals walked 20 safe paces behind!) But I do know that, for now, she seems to enjoy this school game as much as I do.

She brings out the flash cards, aptly prepared and laminated by my mother. I love this game because I am good at it. She flashes word after word, squealing in delight when I confidently recognize the difficult double consonant sounds. I let the words roll off my tongue with a flourish, delighting in each new card and hungry for the challenge of the next one. I know I am going to love school already. My career as a lifelong learner begins.

May 1980

I am 17 years old.

I am living at home with a loving and supportive family. At this point in time, my life is busy but balanced. I take my grade 10 piano; I play in senior and stage bands at school; I train 30 hours a week with a provincial-level coach. My love of learning has continued throughout high school; I earn academic awards for high standards and graduate as an Ontario scholar.

By most accounts, I have been blessed with enough talent to go farther in the sport of synchronized swimming, and I decide that I want to go to the farthest point I can possibly reach. I am determined first to make the Canadian national team. Hard work is nothing to me because I am totally and completely in love with my sport. My parents and friends sense the overwhelming intensity of this desire and support me, even though they realize this means taking a few large risks.

The two national team coaches are in Montreal and Calgary. I talk to both of them in May at the Nationals, and each of them comes to see me train. I must now make the most important decision of my life. After deliberating for a long time, the decision is finally made to go to Calgary, soon to be the high-performance training center for many different sports. I know it is farther from home, and I have to make the commitment to move whether or not I make the team. The coach tells me that I can come and try out . . . but there are no guarantees. Yet, I also know that this coach is one of the best coaches, if not *the* best coach, in the world. She has already produced several world champions. She is tough and determined. She has very high standards. She is a great deal like me.

In early August, I load up the car with my belongings, and with the help and caring of my parents, we make the long trek out west. I have no idea whether or not I have been accepted into the university and have no place to live. All I know is that I am finally going after my dream.

Nothing had ever been as important or as all-consuming as swimming, and nothing ever would be again.

Spring 1985

I retired from active competition in 1985. There were no more Olympic trials, no more world championships, no more chances to travel the world doing what I loved more than anything. It was over . . . and a very special and unique part of me died with it. This was the beginning of my journey to hell and back. I made the trip innumerable times, always living in the victim stance. My eating disorder reached a peak of brutal intensity. I truly believed I was losing my mind.

May 1985 4:21 P.M.
Today I think I am insane,
The general public in my brain,
Tighten . . .
A grip so livid with tension,
That the air refuses to enter
The compressed capsule of a lung,
Which has been stretched to the limit,
Beyond human frame.
Today I think I am insane,
A million thoughts and weird intentions,
Strive to grasp the air,
Yet in despair,
Are smashed and broken like crystal glass.
So tired of fighting this all again,
Today I think I am insane.

I am amazed that my parents allowed me to continue living at home during this time, as I filled myself and everyone around me with a poisonous, bitter energy. Between them they had over 70 years of experience in teaching and education, more than enough to understand fully the value of patience. But I pushed that patience to the limit. There were many sleepless nights for my mother, who worried constantly that I would decide that I couldn't take it anymore and want to end my life. This was a very realistic possibility. It was the one and only time in my life that I totally gave up, that I quit trying. As I reflect on this time now, I see that they were modeling the most difficult kind of teaching—letting someone you care about struggle on their own. They loved and supported me, but they intuitively knew that there exists a line to which we can bring people. And it is a line they must learn to cross for themselves.

The gates of change and learning are often unlocked from within, and to try and save anyone from their struggle is to deprive them of the knowledge and growth that they were meant to get from it in the first place. I spent time with every potential type of help I could think of, from individual psychiatric treatment to support groups to heavy-duty antidepressants. The only person I didn't ask for help was myself. I didn't think I had the strength, resources, or ability to solve my problems. When I retired from swimming, I felt that any sense of "I" had been completely erased and that what remained was a hollow shell, which I constantly tried to fill by training, bingeing, and starving. This did not work. What remained was a complete spiritual void, a seemingly bottomless pit filled with anger, depression, bitterness, and what I felt was a deep, venomous, and well-earned self-hatred.

After all, I had failed to live up to my expectations. Not a big surprise, since I was an expert at the perfectionist's game of constantly setting my standards higher, thereby ensuring that I would never be satisfied.

I felt cheated, as though God had deserted me by removing the most passionate part of my life and leaving me with nothing. At the time, I did not realize that the truth was that I hadn't learned the meaning of appreciation. I didn't know how lucky I had been to have had the opportunity to pursue my dreams to their fullest potential—a chance that many people never get.

I felt as if a bomb had gone off in my life, and there I was, the sole physical survivor, walking through the devastated emotional landscape picking up piece after piece.

The only problem was, I didn't know which pieces were important anymore . . . or how to make sense of putting my life together in any meaningful way. I had no idea at the time that this type of positive disintegration was a necessary part of my transformation. In fact, it was only because things had come so far apart that I would eventually be able to find a new way to see myself, a new way to be. This was certainly no Band-Aid solution. It was a new framework, a totally new perspective.

Learning to Heal: Finding the Miracle for Myself

I have had many important teachers in this respect. The first was my own pain, depression, and fight to recover from a debilitating and dangerous eating disorder. The second was Viola Fodor. I met Viola at a time in my life when the universe had decided that perhaps I had suffered enough and it was time for me to get off my butt and start moving forward. Although I am not a fatalist, I truly believe that the problems and people we are meant to learn from are brought into our lives at the precise moment we need them. We discover that often our greatest opportunities are brilliantly disguised as impossible situations. At this point in my life, I was in desperate need of emotional and spiritual guidance and I am quite certain that I would not be alive today had I not met Viola. My readiness to take the learning from my experiences had been primed by previous failures to help myself get well. I had nothing to lose anymore. I went for help.

Viola believes we all have the potential to help ourselves, no matter what our situation or life story. We merely need to learn how to get out of our own way and to stop playing out our own drama. She had healed her own life years ago by using a holistic therapy approach that emphasized quieting the mind and true reflection. Since that time, she had quietly but successfully been treating eating disorders and depression for years. This in itself is quite a miracle, considering the very grim statistics and often depressing prognoses that many sufferers of eating disorders receive.

I have since come to believe that finding a miracle for ourselves is simply a matter of clarifying our vision and learning to see the uncommon in the common. The paradox of pain, she said, is that my depression itself was there to teach me, that my own experience contained enough information for me to learn to help myself. She was the first person to teach me that I could choose to recover completely. I would not have to cope with food issues, a distorted body image, and spiritual devastation for the rest of my life. The most important key to my healing process was solitude, quiet time, and space.

I have since found that the normal school life does not promote this type of downtime. In fact, the hustle and bustle of a detail-driven day often leaves very little time for reflection. It is extremely unfortunate that while there is a great deal of value in becoming involved in social interaction and trying new activities, we have, as a culture, seriously undervalued the powers available to us in our time alone—the powers to heal, to grow, to learn, and to change ourselves fundamentally in deep and lasting ways. Without learning to take this time, I would not be the person I am today. I would not have the same value system; I would not be able to handle a challenging and busy life; I would not be alive.

March 1992

Having learned the hard way that quieting the mind is an essential life skill, I decide to try and teach it to a grade 12 health class. This is an experiment, I think, knowing that training the mind to think this way can take years and that all I have is a 40-minute period. I book the archive library. With mahogany walls, a warm fireplace, and ancient texts surrounding us, it is the most aesthetic and receptive room for a session like this. My associate teacher has given me the period to experiment and will not be at this lesson. I explain to my class that this time must be approached with an open mind and that they may be uncomfortable at first. It is difficult to run from class to class and then suddenly slow down. A few heads nod in agreement, and the cynics say nothing. I lower the lights and put on some soft music by Chopin, one of my favorites for soothing the soul.

For 20 minutes we lie on the floor, saying nothing, thinking nothing, trying to calm our racing minds. I say to myself, If anyone looked in on this room right now, they would think I am crazy. "What a lunatic student teacher." "What a waste of time." "She will never get a job." I calm myself by remembering that I believe this is important and that no one was ever fired for being creative and innovative or for taking an original risk.

The music ends. I slowly raise the lights. The girls' reactions are widely varied. Some feel it was completely illogical and a waste of time. Most are refreshed and cannot believe they do not do this every day for themselves already. I am asked for tapes of the music and books to read on solitude. We talk for a while longer, then leave a few minutes early so that none of us has to rush off to the frenzied mania of a high school hallway before we are ready. I let the doubters go early, too, and they leave, firmly clasping their books. I am reminded this approach is not for everyone. All of our lessons are different, but teaching well means opening minds to possibilities and then letting each individual choose what suits her best.

I close the library door, refreshed and ready to rejoin the boisterous, laughing students in the hallway. I let their wondrous, buoyant energy wash over me, rejuvenate me, and I smile to myself.

This was a good experiment.

And so my recovery continued. People told me afterward they wished they had videotaped my face before and after my recovery. There was such a remarkable difference in my eyes as I became more and more of my real self. I was seeing things from a much different place, and it showed.

The one positive credit I should give to my temporary and relatively useless bout with psychiatry was that my psychiatrist convinced me to go back to school. I had vowed upon retiring from synchronized swimming that I would never go to university again, probably as a small rebellion against what had been expected of me for as long as I could remember. It wasn't that I didn't love learning. In fact, I had been a voracious reader throughout my healing process, seeking out books and articles on everything from medicine to philosophy, theology, and humor. I was learning the true meaning of the term *active learning,* and I was taking more responsibility for my own lessons. I had loved words—both writing and reading them—even before I went to school.

Guided Self, Self as Guide

The journey toward a greater sense of self is not unlike a trek through unknown mountainous territory. In a situation like this, I knew I did not want a Sherpa guide who had read about the paths in a book. I needed someone who had been there themselves, someone who knew where to find water and shelter, how to pace themselves through difficult storms, which tools were essential to carry in my backpack and which ones should probably be left behind. I had to sense that this person would allow me to travel at my own speed, taking risks when I was ready and resting when necessary. At a time when I no longer believed in myself, I needed a guide who would believe in me and the inner resources we all can possess.

This was quite a leap in faith, as outwardly I had no easily visible or tangible skills to help myself at all. To this day I find it curious that there is no such expression as a step in faith. While it is crucial to take small steps, the act of leaping is a much more accurate description of the buoyant, courageous, and terrifying experience that learning to trust yourself can be. Fortunately, I found a spiritual guide who had taken that leap for herself, a teacher who understood how important it is to move forward even though we don't yet see where we will get the strength to do so.

October 1991

I sit in the biology lab in the middle of my first practice teaching block.

School has been over for a while, and I should be heading home to plan my lesson for tomorrow, a lesson on which I am to be evaluated.

I am exhausted and stressed, and more than a bit distraught about the excess chalk dust now gracing my black dress pants. I suppose "chalkboarding without personal injury" is a new skill I'll have to learn at the faculty.

At the back of the room a young woman sits quietly. I met Sara at the beginning of the year at an eating disorders workshop where I was speaking about recovery. I found out she was attending the school where I was placed for my first session. Sara is bulimic and anorexic. She is currently surviving on Diet Coke and consuming excessive quantities of Prozac and sleeping pills. Her face is closed and drawn, and her exhausted body crumples itself meekly onto a lab stool. She is too tired to go on.

Sometimes I feel as though I could drown in the sadness pervading her eyes, but I know I will not. I have lived this sadness; I understand its rhythm, its depth, its overwhelming ability to incapacitate. But I am not there anymore, and Sara knows this.

Were it not for the fact that I understood her so well, I might have felt better referring her to an expert. After all, I was pretty busy with the new responsibilities of teaching classes. And then I remembered the fear of my own mountain and the kind of teacher I sought to guide my inner journey.

I heave the kind of deep personal sigh that can only come from our true responsibilities and settle into a chair beside her, leaving the science glassware to be cleaned later.

She looks up at me, between wracking sobs, holding onto my belief in her like a lifeline, waiting for courage to move. After a bit, I look up at the lab clock and see an hour of precious time has gone by. I should be going, taking care of business for the next day. And yet I stay, wanting to shake her to the core, wanting to tell her to get on her feet, to move, to risk. I know she can choose to get up eventually, but she doesn't know this and is afraid to do anything but sit with her pain. She has not yet learned that courage follows strength borne of weakness. And so we sit, talk, share our lives for a moment.

After a while, she is calmer, picks up her books, and gets ready to leave. I pack my bag with its relevant curriculum material, and suddenly it seems uncharacteristically light. No one is in the school at this hour, and as I walk down the empty hall to my car, the sound of my dress shoes clicking along keeps me company. There is still planning to do for tomorrow, but it feels somehow less urgent that I prepare a spectacular lesson on which to be judged. I know Sara and I are at the beginning of a long learning process. It would be unethical and impossible for me to open such a personal door, let the breeze flow through for a moment, and then leave her there to walk through alone and unguided. But I don't mind this. It renews my own faith in the process.

She will learn to become more and more of her real self, and I will learn what it really means to be a good teacher.

Learning to Play

As a result of my early positive experiences, I learned that play is an important component of any type of meaningful learning. It is probably because of this realization, combined with a love of physical activity, that I decided to study physical and health education. It was at university that I met another very significant teacher, the man who would eventually share my life and become my life partner.

Paul is a vibrant and effervescent person who also has exceptional listening skills. We hit it off because of what we didn't have in common as much as what we did. At the time we could never have known that we were both destined for the teaching profession; however, I always believed he would be a great teacher simply by what I had learned from him myself. For many years, during the early part of my recovery, I did not smile or laugh. I had completely lost my sense of humor. Paul was an expert at bringing this aspect back to life. He told me I didn't have enough toys and showed me it was important to be silly now and then. He treated me with gentleness, empathy, compassion, and the occasional kick in the butt—all of which I needed at various times during my recovery.

Paul attended teacher's college 2 years before me, all the while doubting whether or not he was the "right type of person" to be a teacher. I wondered how common this static definition of what it means to be a teacher was in preservice training. His perception changed as the year went on as he began to define and develop his own personal teaching style. When I attended the faculty, I, too, found a huge amount of diversity in the teacher candidates, not only in their background, interests, personality, and philosophies of education but also in the reasons and motivations they had for becoming teachers.

My belief that good teaching requires us to offer something of ourselves was strengthened here, as I saw the breadth of gifts that people had to offer, all of them valid, different, and unique. It was like holding up a mirror to the classrooms I was about to face. I was encouraged that I did not feel I had to fit in to a certain mold, that I could be myself and allow my students permission and space to do the same. I saw this work beautifully in Paul's classroom as he grew and refined his own teaching. We continue to learn together about this teaching game. It is an ongoing process. And, fortunately for me, I am sharing it with a kind, loving, and understanding partner who continues to make me laugh and to show me how important it is to have fun.

August 1994

I am sitting at our wedding reception having had the kind of day that exceeded all of our dreams and expectations. My blessings are overflowing in this moment, and I feel it on the deepest level.

I have never felt stronger, more powerful, or more beautiful, and for the first time in years I know that it has nothing to do with what I look like.

I glance over at Viola, who looks vibrant and gorgeous in her fuchsia maid of honor dress. She squeezes my hand knowingly, giving me the inspiration to make my speech. I take a sip of champagne and notice my parents enjoying the wondrous celebration, appreciating what a miracle it is that I have made it to this day—that we have all made it through. I feel I am in slow motion, savoring every morsel of this experience. My life is not perfect, but I have learned to feel joy again, a great achievement in and of itself. My new husband, wonderful and sensitive as ever, sits beside me and takes my hand. It is a strong hand, one that has both caressed and strengthened me.

We have both grown so much, learned so much in the years leading up to this day. I have learned to be genuine, authentic, true to myself and to the process that guides me. Sharing this moment with others who saw the struggle is the best wedding gift I could ever receive. I am so thankful I did not give up. I am so thankful to be alive.

I am so thankful to be myself.

 ## Reflecting, Responding, and Writing

1. Respond to this account of Wendy's professional learning in your own way. How does it make you feel? What does her story cause you to think about? What do you learn about yourself as a teacher?
2. Wendy rediscovered the value of laughter, joy, play, and a sense of humor in her personal and professional lives. Describe the role these qualities play in your life. Describe the ways in which you plan to nurture and develop these qualities.
3. What have you learned about teaching from the negative or painful experiences of your life? How can you use this knowledge to understand yourself as a teacher and to envision the teacher you can become?

4. Having respect for the self and teaching learners to have respect for themselves comprise a significant theme in Wendy's narrative. In your life to date, how have you learned self-respect? How do you maintain and develop your respect for yourself even when you do not live up to your expectations? How do you model respectful relations with students in a classroom setting? How do you teach students to have self-respect and to show respect for others? Describe the ways you work to create a classroom setting that encourages the development of self-respect among students and that nurtures the development of respect for others. Share this writing with a colleague.

5. Wendy learned about compassion through her life experiences. She suggests it is important to treat all students with compassion and empathy. Describe the ways in which you show these qualities in your professional practice. Describe the ways in which you develop these qualities in yourself on an ongoing basis. Describe the ways you can teach students to have compassion for each other. Discuss your ideas with a colleague and document the discussion.

6. Wendy found that solitude, quiet time, and space were necessary for her healing and for personal and professional development. She also noted that schools do not provide these conditions or do not provide emotional and spiritual guidance. How do you respond to this situation as you prepare to teach and be a guide and a leader in the schools of tomorrow? Describe your response in as much detail as you can.

7. Wendy writes about some of her best teachers: her parents, Viola, Sara, and Paul. She explains how she learned in the context of these important relationships with people who were not her teachers in the traditional sense. Identify some of the nontraditional teachers in your life who have taught you important things that you value—parents, grandparents, friends, mentors, family members. Write about each of them separately, describing what you have learned from each of these teachers. Look for the influences of these teachers in your teaching practices, and keep an ongoing record of your observations. Explain how you intend to incorporate these influences more fully into your teaching practices.

8. Read over the writing you have done in response to the narratives in this section. What does the writing tell you about your identity as a teacher? What patterns and/or themes do you see in your writing? What do these patterns or consistent themes tell you about your professional identity? Write about how you will use what you have learned here in your professional practice. Describe your plans for the creation of an authentic professional identity that is true to the person you are and to the person and professional you want to become.

Creating Relationships and Making New Relations: Learning from and with Others

Our world takes off as novel and as distinctly ours precisely in response to how we make new relations of the relations already at work in the environ in which we find ourselves. . . . Helping our children to learn how to make relations is the central and most important task of pedagogy. To the extent that they do not learn to make their own relations, children are doomed to live secondhand lives. They become creatures of habituation who merely follow out the already programmed versions of their experience as inherited from parents, older siblings, and self-appointed definers of reality such as teachers. Ironically, a child who knows how to make relations can convert even authoritarian and repressive treatment into paths of personal liberation, whereas a child who does not make relations converts invitations to free inquiry into derivative and bland repetition. . . . In the hands of those who can make and remake relations, even negative events become the nutrition for a creative life.

J. J. McDermott

The chapters in this section illustrate the ways in which relationships provide the context for professional learning and inquiry. They focus on creating relationships with students and colleagues, and on making new relations between existing ideas and relations in professional education and professional practice. The prospective teachers here explore the ways in which relationships with others have provided a framework in which they have learned throughout their lives, in which

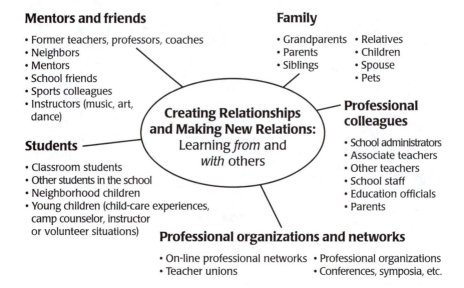

Mentors and friends

• Former teachers, professors, coaches
• Neighbors
• Mentors
• School friends
• Sports colleagues
• Instructors (music, art, dance)

Students

• Classroom students
• Other students in the school
• Neighborhood children
• Young children (child-care experiences, camp counselor, instructor or volunteer situations)

Family

• Grandparents • Relatives
• Parents • Children
• Siblings • Spouse
  • Pets

Creating Relationships and Making New Relations: Learning *from* and *with* others

Professional colleagues

• School administrators
• Associate teachers
• Other teachers
• School staff
• Education officials
• Parents

Professional organizations and networks

• On-line professional networks • Professional organizations
• Teacher unions   • Conferences, symposia, etc.

their identities have been formed, and in which they now engage in professional learning. They describe how they have learned what they know, showing how their professional learning is deeply embedded in personal patterns and ways of knowing and being. They explore the ways in which the knowledge of these patterns provides them with a framework for learning how to create relationships with students and colleagues. The details of their inquiries provide insights regarding how they learned about such diverse issues as choosing among teaching strategies, dealing with the organization and presentation of subject material, administering the details of classroom management, and directing their ongoing professional growth.

The narratives in these chapters show how these prospective teachers learned to understand teaching and learning as primarily relational endeavors. Their accounts explore the ways in which they have learned *from* and *with* other people and from a wide variety of sources. They show how they have reflected on their past experiences and used the knowledge gained to learn what they need to know about creating professional relationships with students and colleagues. They describe their efforts to sense and address students' needs; to win their respect, trust, and allegiance; and to identify teaching strategies that support student dialogue, interaction, and collaborative meaning making.

The prospective teachers featured here explore ways to emphasize inclusiveness, mutuality, reciprocity, empathy, and understanding in their teaching. They show their efforts to create learning communities in which the "I" of individual agendas becomes an attitude of "We." Contracts are replaced by commitments, competition is replaced by collaboration, and individualistic purposes, values, and agendas are replaced by shared values. These beginning teachers deal with the ongoing struggle to find a balance between structure and freedom—enough structure to provide a scaffolding for students' learning, and enough freedom to enable students to develop the skills, understandings, and capacities for active participation in a democratic classroom and society. Their narratives show the details of these struggles and the joys of achieving small successes in the ongoing journey of professional growth.

The idea that we come to know ourselves and construct our professional identities through dialogue, conversations, and interactions with others is supported by the work of researchers and practitioners. Witherall and Noddings (1991) explain that genuine dialogue can take place, and empathy, inclusiveness, mutuality, and trust can develop within "caring relations." Prospective teachers can develop these sensibilities and qualities when they are willing to foster reciprocal relationships with students and colleagues and to move beyond the limitations of their own knowing and ways of being. Within authentic relationships, and through dialogue, discussion, and interaction with the perspectives of others, learners can find the structures in which to define and solve the difficulties, problems, and dilemmas of professional learning and practice, and come to know in new ways.

When teaching is understood as a relational endeavor, the role of the teacher shifts from that of an "all-knowing" individual to that of a learner whose mind and heart are open to new perspectives and whose knowledge is always being remade. Teacher-student relationships based on authority, superiority, and power are replaced by those based on respect, reciprocity, mutuality, care, and trust. These relationships are based on a high degree of responsiveness to the other, on acknowledging and respecting the voices of others, and on showing respect for others' ideas, purposes, motivations, personal agendas, and knowledge. Relationships such as this provide a context for understanding students' perspectives, motivations, and needs and for winning their allegiance and commitment to the curriculum, to the teacher-student relationship, and to the classroom and school communities.

In chapter 6, George Haddad's narrative explores learning about teaching by examining what has been learned within significant teaching-learning relationships in the past. George describes how he uses and adapts this knowledge in the context of his relationships with students, and he addresses the following issues:

- Acknowledging and identifying what has been learned about teaching from significant teacher-learner relationships in the past (learning how to teach for student engagement)
- Recognizing the value of authenticity, caring, trust, respect, and inspiration in teacher-student relationships

- Honoring the relationship between subject matter and students' lives (Mathematics and science are vehicles for the development of curiosity about how things work and the reasons why things are the way they are in the natural world.)
- Acknowledging and valuing difference and diversity—adapting teaching to address understanding of student difference.

In chapter 7, Gilbert Barsky's narrative focuses on making new relations between ideas, insights, and practices from the perspective of a prospective teacher. Gilbert's narrative addresses these issues:

- Learning about teaching from life's experiences as a parent, a sports enthusiast, an employee, and a student
- Understanding teaching from the teacher's perspective and making connections between personal knowledge and professional knowledge
- Learning to relate to students in ways that nurture the teacher-learner relationship, to promote student engagement with subject matter, and to stimulate and inspire learning
- Making connections between the person and the professional—compassion, care, humor, and creativity in the development of professional knowledge and professional practice

In chapter 8, Ellen Shifrin discusses the creation of authentic relationships with students as the basis for good teaching. Ellen's narrative deals with these issues:

- Building trust, reciprocity, and mutual regard in relationships with students as a basis for student inquiry and personal meaning making
- Learning about teaching by observing students' learning processes (learning from and with students by paying attention to the dynamics of the relationship and to the processes of students' learning)
- Connecting the body and the mind
- Valuing the body's ways of knowing
- Learning by connecting with self and with others, connecting internal and external knowledge, and re-forming what is known in the light of new understandings

In chapter 9, Alicia Cashore's narrative emphasizes reflective practice as the basis for the development of professional knowledge. Alicia shows the dialectical relationship between theory and practice. Her narrative deals with the following issues:

- Relating practice to theory and theory to practice so that they support and enrich each other
- Regarding reflective practice and inquiry as a framework for making new relations among ideas, theories, people, and practical actions

- Relating to students, classroom situations, and social contexts in new ways by learning teaching practices that are appropriate to the context, culture, and learners' needs
- Perceiving curriculum as the interaction among teacher, student, and subject matter
- Fostering interactive learning through collegial relationships with experienced colleagues—sharing stories, agendas, and priorities—adapting and enhancing knowledge and capacity for action
- Making connections among professional practices, school priorities, and students' learning
- Incorporating technology into the classroom

CHAPTER 6

Some Experiences of a Lifelong Learner: Teachers I Have Known

From the very beginning of his education a child should experience the joy of discovery. The discovery which he has to make is that general ideas give an understanding of that stream of events which pours through his life, which is his life.

A. N. WHITEHEAD

George Haddad's narrative illustrates the way knowledge is created and shaped within relationships. This understanding helps him to learn about teaching and about becoming the kind of teacher he wants to be. George explores what he has learned about teaching and learning in the context of his relationships with significant teachers in his life. He recognizes these relationships as the sources for his image of a teacher as an inspirational, caring, and responsive guide. This image structures his ongoing inquiry, helps him to interpret his current teaching practices, and directs his efforts to learn how to be the kind of teacher who continually nurtures and inspires his students. His narrative supports Albert Einstein's statement that imagination is more important than knowledge and that the stimulation of the student's imagination is one of the teacher's most important tasks regardless of the subject matter.

George's narrative describes his efforts to create teaching-learning relationships where students are treated with respect, where genuine creativity is fostered and lifelong learning is nurtured. George shows that by listening to students—their stories, concerns, perspectives, dilemmas, and uncertainties—in the context of authentic relationships, he learns how to reach and teach them. Recognizing that students' attitudes toward school and school subjects are connected to the whole of their lives, he acknowledges the necessity for adaptability and flexibility in these relationships and in his teaching methods. He comes to understand that the purpose of his teaching is to help students to build self-esteem, to enable them to "see patterns of meaning in their learning," and to develop a love of learning and the habits of lifelong learning.

George uses his understandings of cross-cultural settings and of cultural and linguistic differences among people to be responsive to students' differences in the multicultural environment of the schools in which he does his practice teaching. He draws on his experience as a minority Arab student in a Jewish university and on his relationship with a teacher there who exemplified impartiality, authenticity, and genuine caring. His reflections on this experience enable him to articulate his belief in the importance of inspiration, accommodation, and adaptation in teacher-student relationships. He shows his efforts to acknowledge and value difference and diversity in his classroom practices. He shows also how he makes connections between the science-based knowledge of the academic subjects of science and math and the personal and interpersonal knowledge gained in life experiences. George relates these new understandings to his instructional strategies and professional practices, and he explains that a good teacher needs subject knowledge, interpersonal knowledge, and social, cultural, and pedagogical knowledge. He shows how the intellect, the emotions, and the imagination are linked in the processes of learning, describing the teacher's role in creating an environment where these links are acknowledged, valued, and enacted.

The Caring Professional

by George Haddad

He was in his seventies when I became aware of his presence.

He always had a red tarboosh on, and when he took it off, I could notice that he was almost completely bald. Those who sat in his company felt an air of serenity and tranquility about him.

His walk was always slow and steady, reflecting a man full of integrity, sure of himself, confident, conscious of his surroundings, and aware of the people who come across him.

His face was calm, invariably smiling, radiating love and friendship. He was honest, sincere, trustworthy, and respectable. My grandfather was a merchant by profession, a pious man, a preacher in the local church in our small village. He made the habit of coming to our home every Sunday afternoon. Being exact about his time, he would arrive at a certain hour. I, a child 6 years of age, would wait for him anxiously at the gate to greet him, for he was my most beloved grandfather.

(Professional Journal, 1995)

As I reflect on the growth of my professional knowledge, I become increasingly aware of the way in which the vast array of people I encountered during my upbringing—including my teachers—has shaped my conception and understanding of the teaching profession. Many of my past experiences have made me aware that the essence of learning is to acquire a broader view of the world around me, to discover new things. It is this awareness that has characterized my commitment to becoming a teacher.

Although I formed my first image of a good teacher in the early stages of my schooling, that image continued to change and develop as I moved on to secondary school and later as I encountered professors and teachers at the university level. During the past year at the faculty of education, my own image of the professional teacher has undergone a restructuring as I have learned more about secondary school students, the schools themselves, and school systems.

As a child, I believed that a teacher was not simply the person who stood in front of a group of kids in a classroom teaching them how to read, write, and count. In our small village, a teacher was anybody in the community who could grab my attention, who was charismatic, who could tell fascinating stories, and who could let my imagination soar beyond the boundaries of the real world. For me, a teacher was someone who made me curious about how things work and the reasons why they are the way they are. I had many "teachers"—in the literal sense of the word—who taught me in a classroom environment, but unfortunately they are not the people who stick in my mind. I usually forgot them sooner or later.

My Grandfather as Teacher

One person who made a great impression on me as a child happened to be my grandfather. In his company, I would forget about my toys and my friends and would listen, mesmerized, to his stories. My grandfather was like a sculptor who carved and molded my imagination. His teaching made me think, question, and reflect.

My grandfather was a good storyteller. As he sat there in his armchair, he would narrate the stories of his youthful past in exquisite detail, stories from a time when the Turks were in control of Palestine. Being a merchant, he would tell us of his adventures, his travels from Galilee to the city of Beirut, when donkeys and horses were the only means of transportation. He always captivated the attention of all who listened to him. He spoke with the grace and eloquence of a man of letters, taking his time, making sure that his story had a well-thought beginning, an interesting climax, and an appropriate ending. My grandfather's stories fascinated and delighted his audience.

For me, his stories were of immense value, enriching my imagination and training me to be reflective at an early stage. And it was not only the stories themselves that captured my attention. My grandfather was also good at mathematics. Although his formal schooling ended in grade 3, he had acquired the basic skills through self-interest and self-inquiry. On Sunday afternoon there were occasions when he would ask me to perform simple arithmetic and he would pose problems to me in a way that was entertaining. Everything was casual, and at the time I did not feel as if I were doing any learning. He would challenge me with a problem with a big smile on his face, and I would accept his challenge with much enthusiasm and great interest.

(Professional Journal, 1995)

As I reflect on the impact my grandfather had on my life, I think that teachers who have a long-lasting effect on their students possess certain qualities of a higher order that transcend mere knowledge of content. Teachers must be people full of integrity and sure of their own values. They must demonstrate confidence and optimism. Students look for those characteristics because they constantly look for their ideal. Young people are drawn to older adults because of their loving nature and friendliness. Young people treasure a friendship with an adult who they think is unique, and they will learn from such a person.

Because of his advanced knowledge compared to many of his fellow men in the village, people would come and seek my grandfather's advice, or to ask him to read a letter they couldn't decipher for themselves.

He volunteered to teach mathematics to my class in the private school that belonged to our Anglican church. He would come every morning to the school and would tell the children a story with a lesson behind it and then would conduct a prayer before students went to their different classrooms. He was able to teach our class first thing in the morning and then leave to go about his business. He took on the responsibility of teaching a whole class for 2 years.

(Professional Journal, 1995)

Children often read between the lines and draw conclusions about the adults in front of them, about their honesty, their sincerity, and their approachability. They observe what adults do rather than listening to what they say. Young people do not distinguish between university graduates and nongraduates; they don't care about titles, and they don't respect a particular teacher simply because he or she possesses more knowledge. Teachers are respected by their students when, at the same time as they convey knowledge, they also show their human side. Teachers must show they care about their students' well-being, about their overall growth, and about their unknown, distant future. Trustworthy teachers must always have students' futures in mind and must always keep focused on the knowledge, attitudes, and tools they'll need when they're no longer under the teachers' supervision or surveillance.

My grandfather was such a teacher. While he was living his last years on Earth, he had a vision for me. He planted in me the seeds of learning, he invested in my imagination, and he equipped me with the proper tools to face the future. Those tools were not sophisticated, computerized, or technologically advanced. They were the tools of humanity: friendship, love, kindness, and self-inquiry. My grandfather was not a "professional" teacher as such. He did not obtain a teaching certificate from a college; he even did not graduate from elementary school. Despite his background, he was by instinct a good teacher and a conscientious educator.

My grandfather died of a heart attack while sitting on a bench in the church he had loved most, listening to a young priest full of spirit and enthusiasm. I was 10 years old then. For me, the world seemed to come to an abrupt end, for my grandfather personified everything good in this world.

He was, after all, my very best teacher ever.

Perhaps it is because of my grandfather that I am who I am.

(Professional Journal, 1995)

Guidance and Growth: Teacher as Nurturer

I love to walk in the woods among trees. I think these trees have a lot to teach us. They are forever growing toward the highest heights—this is their ultimate goal. Trees withstand the harsh winter and put up with the dry, hot summer to reach those heights. They teach people how to seek freedom. While they may begin in a suffocating thicket, they grow toward light, sun, and air. But they can also be stunted by factors that can impede their growth and well-being.

People can be hard on trees. They cut them, twist branches, prune them incorrectly. Trees are voiceless; they don't know how to express their pain.

(Professional Journal, 1995)

A Teacher Is Like a Gardener

During my adolescence, I encountered another important teacher who made a powerful impression on me. This teacher was a young priest in the local church. He became my ideal and my hero because, in my eyes, he possessed all the qualities to which I aspired. He exhibited great enthusiasm in his beliefs, an enthusiasm that he put into practice. His Bible study classes—aimed at young people like myself—were both analytical and inspiring. He always came to class prepared, and he filled the blackboard with detailed analyses. He used elaborate facial expressions and moved his hands in a way that reinforced the meanings of his words. He captured my attention, and I loved to be in his company. He taught me it is easier to make an impact on young people than it is to influence those who are older. But he also used to say, "It is not enough to plant a shrub and water it for a few years. You have to look after it for decades. Only then you can enjoy the fruits of your labor." I would like to dedicate this piece of prose to that young priest:

> Children are like trees. Their goal is to grow, to laugh, to be free, and to reach the heights. They are also fragile like trees. They risk being stunted by the darkness and by the cold, dry soil of the classroom. Or they can be trained into some twisted and perverse shape by a teacher's harsh pruning shears. A tree will grow in a crooked way if we don't care about it when it's still young and easy to bend. Children are like young trees; one can shape their minds and influence their behavior in their early years. And, as they grow, they harden like the branches of an old tree.
>
> Learners are also like trees: they face hardships and difficulties as they aspire to grow. To a student, a teacher is like a gardener. Just as a gardener must constantly look after trees to ensure steady growth, so too must a teacher care for students to ensure unhindered development. A good early foundation for a student is like a good soil for a tree; without it no growth is possible. Like fresh air and water, books constantly give nourishment to the mind and the spirit. We teachers must train our students to value the knowledge found in books and provide guidance to enable them to be conscious of the powers of their own minds.
>
> We teachers are like trees, too. We need to grow and must seek constant nourishment for our minds and our spirit to be able to continue our journey as educators.

> (Professional Journal, 1995)

As a professional teacher, the image of the tree appeals to me because it symbolizes the aspirations of both the teacher and the student. Children, like trees, are prone to being stunted if a teacher doesn't offer the right conditions, the right classroom setting, and a caring relationship in which to learn. They are also vulnerable and powerless. They deserve our constant care and attention. Teachers are both trees and gardeners. In one sense, they are gardeners, ensuring the growth of students; in another sense, they are trees seeking nourishment for their own minds and souls. Their goal is to model lifelong learning for their students and to help students to become lifelong learners also.

Recognizing and Adapting to Difference

I still treasure my special relationship with a fine, impartial Jewish university professor who believed in equality for all students, irrespective of their culture or ethnicity. He was in his late 60s, a knowledgeable biochemistry teacher. To me, this man was unique because he understood the futility of the ethnocultural conflicts that arise in a multicultural society. He made every effort to fight cultural bias and discrimination against the Arab students who studied in his department. He had a penetrating vision, and he always looked beyond the horizon of present reality to a more harmonious coexistence amongst people from different backgrounds. As a minority Arab student in a Jewish university, I looked to my biochemistry professor as my counselor and my adviser. His warmth and his friendship made me feel at ease and he encouraged me to seek his companionship whenever possible. I don't know whether this person is still alive, but, because of his genuine concern for me, I am a better person today. He cared about my future as if I were his only son.

> Our children have the same varied needs as trees. Will we, teachers, be able to provide the help that will satisfy the needs of each individual child? Maybe we still have a lot to learn.
>
> (Professional Journal, 1995)

As a teacher in a secondary school in the Canadian multicultural society, I need to develop attitudes and personal qualities that will encourage peaceful interaction among students of different cultural backgrounds. I need to reinforce my belief that cultural pluralism is a worthy goal and to enhance minority students' positive self-image. As a teacher, I have to be aware that cultural and linguistic differences are positive individual differences and that flexibility in human relations is the key to successful coexistence. The image of my biochemistry teacher remains alive in me and guides my classroom actions and plans for the future.

To Be a Teacher Is to Be a Good Human Being

I have spent a total of 3 years with my graduate supervisor, working in a research lab. In spite of my daily interaction with him, I know very little about him as a person. Our relationship is businesslike and centered around the research project that is our common interest.

He is an extremely dry, cold person. He is egocentric. His main interest is to get fast results in the projects he assigns his students to compete in the scientific arena. My supervisor is well acquainted with his narrow specialty in immunology, but he doesn't know how to communicate either warmth or friendliness to those who work for him. He makes life difficult for others by being watchful, critical, and bossy.

He has no interest in the personal growth and advancement of the people around him. He thinks only of himself and how to compete to achieve fame and success.

I am the father of two children, and, one day, my daughter is ill. I have to stay home to take care of her. The following day I return to work, but my supervisor doesn't bother to ask about my daughter. His philosophy: you leave personal issues at home when you come to work.

The negative experience I have with this man causes me to question my career choice seriously. Then, I remember a saying my mother used to quote from the Bible: everything that happens works toward a greater good.

I believe there is truth in such a belief and am glad to have chosen teaching as my profession.

Ultimately, the lesson I have drawn from my relationship with that supervisor is the importance of treating students as human beings, just like oneself. They have worries, concerns, and stories to tell. They need my friendship and care and understanding more than anything else.

To be a teacher is to be a good human being.

(Professional Journal, 1995)

My year in teacher education has reinforced my belief that my potential would have been wasted if I hadn't chosen the teaching profession as my future career. It has also heightened my awareness of the difficulties and the challenges a beginning teacher encounters in a secondary school setting. I've come to believe that I am equipped to deal with the joys and problems that abound in a classroom and that I am ready to begin my career.

Creating Relationships with Students

In my first practice teaching session, I learned teaching is an art; it requires expertise and humanity. Reflecting back, I can now see that it is not sufficient to be warm and loving toward students, nor is it sufficient to employ teaching practices based solely on intuition, personal preference, or conventional wisdom. In my approach to teaching I have had to incorporate scientific skills and knowledge with my knowledge of humanity and of relationships. I have found that the art of teaching, like most human endeavors, cannot be defined by scientific knowledge alone. It's an art that is dependent upon a complex set of individual judgments based on personal values and beliefs, subject expertise, and knowledge of people.

In my second practice session, I was placed in a school situated in a poor area in Toronto. It was a small school with many problems.

Students' self-esteem was low, and these students found school difficult and irrelevant in terms of their own lives. Many of these students came from unstable family backgrounds and were unmotivated to learn in my classroom. I had to adapt, take charge, and accept the challenge. I was afraid in the beginning, afraid of classroom management problems. However, as I established relationships with the students, taught them, and talked to them, I began to feel their pains and their dilemmas, their uncertainties, and their concerns. Physically, they were growing fast. Intellectually, however, they were poorly skilled swimmers gasping in a turbulent sea of disorganized knowledge and societal pressures. I wanted to help, to teach, to motivate, to inspire.

My experience in the third practice teaching session differed vastly from the second. Students came from stable family backgrounds and the school culture was conducive to learning. Here, I was faced with a different challenge. I was required to show a command of various knowledge bases: academic, pedagogical, social, and cultural. In this school I had the opportunity to apply new teaching strategies such as cooperative learning and investigation. My teaching subject was mathematics, and my role was clearly to help students to see patterns of meaning in their learning and to foster genuine creativity in them.

(Professional Journal, 1995)

My practice teaching experiences have made me aware of difference and diversity and the importance of accommodation and adaptation, as I've tried to meet the regulations of each school and the individual needs of each student. I have learned the importance of being academically capable and of caring about the total well-being of children and youth. I have also learned the importance of constantly motivating students to improve themselves academically, spiritually, emotionally, and socially. For me, these qualities must be accompanied by four other prerequisites for effective teaching in my career:

- A growing *knowledge base* that guides the art of teaching
- An expanding *repertoire* of effective practices from which to draw
- Continuous *reflection* and problem solving
- The firm belief that learning to teach is a *lifelong process*

My philosophy, which is a by-product of my total experiences as a learner, is that my immediate task is to keep students interested in learning, to make them self-conscious of the processes of their own minds, and to urge them to develop all aspects of themselves as human beings—to seek wisdom and grace. I am back to a new beginning: a beginning full of expectations and uncertainties, and ready for the unknown future ahead. I will be calm, wait, hope, and pray a teacher's prayer:

For if I help the world to grow
in wisdom and in grace
then I shall feel that I have won
and have filled my place.

 ## Reflecting, Responding, and Writing

1. How does George's narrative connect to your experience?
   In what ways does it stir your thinking? What is the most
   important thing that George says?
2. George's awareness of how he has learned within relationships
   helps him to reflect on his teaching practices and to plan future
   actions. Identify those individuals who have taught you about
   relationships, and describe what you know. Describe a good
   teacher-student relationship, and identify the qualities that
   exist in such a relationship. Discuss the nature of "love" and
   "care" in the context of the teacher-student relationships.
   Discuss your ideas with a colleague and document your
   discussion. Organize a large-group discussion where you share
   ideas, strategies, and advice about creating good relationships
   with students.
3. George uses the image of the tree to symbolize the aspirations
   of both the teacher and the student and as a metaphor for the
   teacher-student relationship. What image of the teacher-student
   relationship works best for you? Describe this image in as
   much detail as possible.
4. Describe a teacher (or teachers) who influenced you in the way
   that George's grandfather influenced him. Explain how this
   person (or persons) shaped your understandings of teaching
   and learning. Identify the ways you can incorporate these
   positive influences into your current teaching practices.
   Describe your efforts (successes and failures) to enact these
   influences in your classroom practices. Design a plan for
   bringing your ideals and principles closer to your practical
   actions. Accepting that this is a lifelong endeavor, create a
   short-term plan and a long-range plan. Identify the ways you
   will look for progress and growth.
5. George describes his purpose as a math teacher as helping
   students to see patterns of meaning in their learning and to
   foster genuine creativity. Reflect on the purposes you have for

your teaching. Document your reflections and plans for the future.

6. George learned about dealing with cultural bias, discrimination, and ethnocultural conflict through his experiences in a positive relationship with a professor. What personal experiences (if any) have you had as a minority person? What do you know about minority students' experiences of classrooms and schools? How do you respond to cultural and linguistic differences among students in your classroom? How do you acknowledge difference and diversity among students in the ways in which you design and present your lessons? How do you ensure that your classroom is a good learning environment for all students?

7. George articulates a philosophy of teaching that is grounded in relationships and in relational learning. This philosophy enables him to make connections among his personal purposes, his knowledge of science and math, and his knowledge of pedagogy. It enables him to plan his future growth as a relational teacher. Discuss this with a colleague, and write about the ways in which you are making these connections in your own life and in your professional practices. Write about your plans for future growth, professional development, and the development of your abilities to understand and enact your teaching as a relational endeavor. Review the qualities of relational teaching as outlined on page 71, and address them in your plans for your future professional learning.

CHAPTER 7

Making Connections:
Creating New Relationships

The purpose of education is to show a person how to define himself authentically and spontaneously in relation to the world—not to impose a pre-fabricated definition of the world, still less an arbitrary definition of the individual himself.

THOMAS MERTON

Gilbert Barsky's narrative deals with the making and remaking of relations and relationships in his life. Gilbert shows how he learned to "think like a teacher" by revisiting his past experiences from his current perspective as a prospective teacher. Recognizing that his knowledge has been constructed in his roles as student, parent, employee, and citizen, he reassesses these experiences in the light of his new knowledge about students, schools, subject matter, teaching strategies, and professionalism. By exploring the origins of what he knows, Gilbert embarks on an inquiry into the connections between learning and teaching. His narrative shows how he engages in the process of adapting his existing ideas and understandings and of restructuring his knowledge. It provides insights into the way a prospective teacher develops more sophisticated understandings of the dynamics of the teaching-learning relationship and of the conditions within which student learning is stimulated and inspired. It shows the relationship among values, beliefs, and classroom practices, as one beginning teacher makes new relations among existing entities and creates new kinds of relationships with the people around him in classrooms and schools. His narrative shows the multifaceted nature of teachers' knowledge and the way it is adapted, enriched, and transformed through reflection on practice and through continuous inquiry.

At the Beginning

by Gilbert Barsky

My first years at school could hardly be termed an academic success. But I learned some important lessons.

I failed grade 2, but I did not repeat it. There, I finally said it. I have kept this a secret for over 40 years. Perhaps I failed grade 2 because I thought school was supposed to be fun instead of work. I do not blame my grade 2 teacher. It just happened. At the age of 8, I had experienced one of the most significant events in my life.

Naturally, I did not tell my parents. Those days, you were given a report card that you were supposed to bring home. Mine conveniently got lost. I had no plan as to how I would keep this secret from them, but I was in no rush to tell. Then fortune smiled on me.

There was a new building under construction a few blocks from where I lived. One of my friends told me it was a new public school. It would be open in September. I remembered my other first days of school. I checked my impressions out with my friends. There was excitement and confusion everywhere. You went to school and stood in line. They asked you your name, where you lived, what grade were you in last year, and so forth. On the first day of school, I went to this new school instead of my old one. I answered all of the above questions honestly. I was placed in grade 3.

In January, I was told to report to the principal's office. My record had caught up to me and he was not happy, but I told him that I stood third in the class so he let me stay there. That year I passed grade 3!

Although I didn't realize it then, I have come to learn that the grapevine starts at a very early age. I had asked my friends how they thought things happened. I figured out how the system worked. I got around the system.

Today, I realize that always stating the obvious is good insurance in teaching since there might be a younger version of myself out there.

In high school, fortune smiled upon me again. I was put in the class of a superb teacher. When I think of the teacher I would most like to resemble, it is my grade 10 geometry teacher, Mr. Tuck.

It was an ordinary class day in the late fall. Mr. Tuck was not in the room, but the class was working. He had programmed us: in the event that he was not there, we were instructed to work at our desks or do an assignment at the board. That's just what we were doing!

About 5 minutes into the class, Mr. Tuck burst into the room. He picked up two pieces of chalk and proceeded to run around the circumference of the room, drawing two lines around it, making chalk marks on the boards, the doors, the windows, and even across the backs of the students who were in his way. He started and ended at the front center chalkboard. In some places, the two lines came close to each other, but they never met. Then he turned to the class and said, "Well, that's it. That is today's lesson. Everything you need to know. Parallel lines never meet! Any questions?"

Most of my classmates were either too stunned or intimidated to say anything. I raised my hand.

"Sir. Are railway tracks parallel lines?"

"Yes, they are!"

"Well, sir, when you stand in the middle of a set of railway tracks and look down them, they seem to meet way down in the distance."

"At infinity, Barsky?"

"Yes, sir, at infinity. So they do meet somewhere."

There was a dead silence in the class, but only for a very short time.

"Barsky, do you have any idea what happens to math teachers when they die?"

"No, sir."

"When they die, math teachers don't go to heaven. They go to infinity. They are all out there sitting on all those parallel lines. That's why parallel lines meet at infinity! Because all the dead math teachers are sitting on them."

Three decades on, I still haven't ever forgotten that lesson. I accepted his explanation even though I knew intuitively that it wasn't right. Of course, I could not prove him wrong. But I always did my homework throughout the term. Geometry became one of my better subjects.

I felt safe asking Mr. Tuck this question because I felt that my question was a logical, normal one. I had done my homework, so I wasn't nervous. When Mr. Tuck took a tangential line of questioning by asking me where I thought dead math teachers went when they died, I knew I could trust him. He would not embarrass me.

I felt secure in Mr. Tuck's class. His classes were always amusing and interesting, and I always came into that class in the right mind-set. I was in there to learn. My mind was open, and even now I can still remember many other lessons he taught me as if they were yesterday. They were more than factual. They were different and they were entertaining.

Learning from Children

To comprehend who I am as a person and a teacher, I look back at the events that shaped me and taught me what I know.

After leaving university, I got married and had a family—two children, a girl and a boy. For 14 years and 4 months, I had a daughter, until asthma claimed her. She was bright, inquisitive, often vexatious, and also a ray of sunshine in my life.

When Rachel was 2½ years old, a disaster occurred. The television set in our house stopped working. I had removed two fuses from the back and that may have had an influence on its lack of performance. The effect on Rachel was rather staggering, as even at the age of $2\frac{1}{2}$, her perspective on books changed dramatically. She became interested in those strange rectangular items that she saw Mummy and Daddy sticking their noses into for long hours at a time. She began to acquire a library of her own.

It was a delight to have her sit on my lap while we read stories. We covered the usual gambit of children's stories: fairy tales, pictures of animals, dinosaurs, and fun stuff. There was a series of stories which I like to think of as "middle-class bears." These bears played out traditional roles. The father went out and worked. The mother stayed home and kept house. The children played. These bears had very human characteristics. They smoked pipes; they wore pants; they rode bicycles. This all appeared very natural, in those storybooks.

One day, I took my daughter to Canada's Wonderland where a large advertising campaign based around the Smurfs had been mounted. It was rather simple. "Come to Canada's Wonderland and meet the Smurfs." I was walking through the main entrance with my daughter when I saw the life-size, costumed characters. These Smurfs may have fooled a 3-year-old, but not the little boy beside me. I overheard him say in a rather disappointed tone, "Awww. I wanted to see real Smurfs!" The costumed characters did not fool him. He was clearly disillusioned and disappointed.

That little boy's reaction stayed in my mind. A few months later my wife and I were planning to take Rachel to the zoo. We talked about what Rachel was reading, and we both decided to prepare her for the outing. I would tell her that real bears do not go around wearing pants, smoking pipes, or riding bicycles. I sat down with Rachel and told her just that. She listened to me and just accepted it. I never thought any more about it. We all would have lived happily ever after, had it not been for two seemingly unrelated events.

First, the day that we had planned to go to the zoo, it rained! So we canceled. We never did go that year. Second, the Moscow Circus played Toronto four or five months later. One of the joys in being a parent is that it gives you a chance to go to the circus. My wife wanted to have the day off for herself, so I bought tickets for me and Rachel.

My daughter and I traveled from where we lived in Burlington to the big city of Toronto. This was one of her first times going to a public event. There was the usual excitement that goes with a circus—clowns, jugglers, acrobats. I was having a wonderful time watching the show until the trained animal acts started. In came the bears—riding bicycles, wearing pants, smoking pipes. My daughter got quite excited (and loud).

"Look, Daddy. Look. Bears wear pants! Bears ride bicycles! Bears smoke pipes!"

She could hardly wait to get home and tell her mother what she saw at the circus. What did I learn from all this? What I told my daughter, I told her in good faith. I was her authority figure. I told her what I honestly believed to be true, without malice or any evil intent. I never considered all the permutations of what I was excluding. They were so remote that they just never entered my head. She saw I was wrong. With that event, which she never let me forget, she was able to chip away at my credibility.

As a teacher, I have to be very careful to use a qualifier. There are no absolute truths anymore. Marriages and homes suddenly fall apart. Stars are exposed as being killers, drug addicts, child molesters, or not even the actual singers.

We ask children to perform a difficult task—to listen. Many adults do not do this very well. We tell children fairytales and other stories to get their minds active and running. There are all those fresh ideas just waiting to bud. When they want to ask questions, they sometimes interrupt us. What is going on inside their minds? What message do they get when we do not acknowledge the value in what they ask or say? I suspect that when they are devalued in this way, what children learn is how to tune out. They are physically there, but they do not participate. They are merely learning how to endure.

I see this happening in the classroom. Some children can be both silent and listening. Some are simply tuned out. They are silent, but nothing active is going on inside their heads. When they are actively listening, then their minds are active. How strange it is that as teachers in classrooms, we ask them to listen to us, but we spend so little time really listening to them.

I find it interesting that the same letters are present in the words silent and listen. They mean such different things. It all depends on how they are arranged. I am very careful now how I arrange things in my classroom. As both a teacher and a parent, I try to act as a role model. Everything that my pupils see and hear has an impression on them. It is not easy to camouflage personal values.

When my son was about 3½ years old, he was very observant. Like any other youngster, he watched his parents. I do not believe that children have their place, that they should be seen and not heard. My belief is that they should be treated like young learners.

One day, an old friend dropped in to visit in the middle of the afternoon. As teenagers, we had played a lot of checkers and chess together. Playing these games provided us with a vehicle to discuss our inner feelings and to just enjoy each other's company. So my friend and I sat in the living room and played four or five games of checkers. We talked. We laughed a lot. It was good to share his company again. While we were doing that, my son played quietly at the other end of the living room.

After my friend left, my son said, "Play with me, Daddy." That is always a pleasant request, so I asked him what he wanted to play. He pointed to the checkerboard and checkers, and said, "That."

"Do you know how to play?"

He said, "Yes." I assumed that my wife had taught him, so I set up the board and we started. He did not stay on the right colored square the first time. I simply chalked that up to undeveloped muscle coordination of a 3-year-old. He got the next few moves right. Then it came to a time when I had to jump one of his men. I did. When I did that, he had a strange look on his face. It was a combination of confusion and a bit on the hurt side. He said nothing. It happened again, with the same results, but not quite as hurt this time. Then he looked out the window and said, "Look Daddy, it's snowing." As this was late September, I was a little surprised. When I looked out the window, I could not see any snow. When I looked back at the board, one of my checkers was gone. He had placed it on the side of the board, in the same fashion as I had done when I had taken off one of his pieces. It happened again, only with a slightly different distraction on his part, and I lost another checker.

The game soon lost any resemblance to the formal game of checkers. We would take turns playing distraction; sometimes one of the other player's checkers would disappear from the board. But I noticed that he never got ahead of me: he was very careful to take turns. He never took two turns in a row, either in moving or in removing the pieces, and he worked very hard at keeping the conversation going. He had a lot of fun moving the pieces around. He was able to comprehend the concept of a "kinger" and really enjoyed moving his pieces around. After a while, it became very frustrating to me. There was no way this game could be won. We were just pushing pieces around the board. Fortunately, my wife came home and said it was time for dinner. My son quit right then and there. So did I.

Later I asked my wife if she had taught him checkers. She said, "No." Looking back on that, I realize how logical his actions were. He saw his father having a good time "playing" with a friend of his. He just wanted to imitate his father. He, too, wanted "to play" with someone. He had observed our actions and told a little white lie regarding his experience. We did have a good time playing his form of the game, with his type of rules. He just wanted to play. Winning and formal rules were concepts that he had yet to be exposed to. As a child, playing meant taking turns and making sure that everyone is treated equally and that no one's feelings are hurt.

Often I think, "At what stage in life did I stop playing to play and start playing to win?" How quick it is that the object of our games stops being to have fun and becomes to win at any cost. I don't think my son was more than 5 before this message had been firmly implanted in his mind. Games are merely simulations of life. So much of what we imprint on our children contains a winner and loser theme. My son, in that checker game, had already worked out a better system. Both of us were having fun. There were no losers under his system. We were both winners. I frequently wonder whether I taught him a useful lesson when I showed him all those "winning strategies" during his later years. Wouldn't it be nice if schools and the world were set up so we could exist using his rules for checkers?

Learning from Life

During my year in a teacher education program, I sometimes recalled the old saying "Good teachers make up lesson plans. Great teachers steal them." I learned a lot about the instructional process from my observations of how learning happens in life—on vacation, at work, or at play. I learned something about teaching from my experiences learning to ski.

Skiing is a weird sport. You go up to the top of a high mountain. You strap two long boards to your feet. Then you go hurtling down at the speed of a car. When you reach the bottom alive, you go right back up to the top of the mountain again! It takes a lot of training and lessons to master downhill skiing.

When I went on winter vacations, my family came with me. We all took lessons. The adult classes were very sophisticated at the advanced levels. I learned about momentum, angulation, downhill weighting, and lots of other complex concepts. It worked. However, the lesson that impressed me the most was when I listened to my children being taught.

The instructor told my children that they had a magic eye, right in the center of their chest. The instructor pointed to a spot where the sternum is located. What the instructor told them was that wherever they pointed their magic eye, that was where the rest of their body would follow. If a skier crouched over, with their chest angled downward, then the magic eye would be looking at the snow, and they would wind up falling. If they stood tall and always pointed their magic eye down the hill, then they would be able to ski down the hill. This method works. There is no magic to it. If a skier's upper body is positioned right, it is difficult to fall or go wrong.

This taught me a lesson about the complicated way that many adults relay instructions. What my children's instructor told them was simple and brilliant. Why can't adults teach other adults so simply? Why do we make learning so complex? I try to treat all of my pupils (adults and not-so-old young adults) as if they are children. First I give them the simple version, so at least they know where they are headed. Later, I can add the extra technical jargon, if they need it.

It is very hard work to make a lesson simple and uncomplicated. It takes analytical, introspective, complicated thoughts, to make complex concepts sound simple. I often think about a comment one professor wrote at the end of a 20-page letter to a colleague. "I am sorry to have written you such a long letter, but I did not have the time to write a short one." After a few years now of preparing lessons, I know how true this is.

I learned significant lessons about the value of friendship, of self-confidence, of motivation through my experiences with Mensa. I can still recall the first time I read about it in a classic comic book when I was a teenager. I was very impressed. I had this image of intellectuals sitting around discussing Einstein's theory of relativity, arguing about Plato's Republic, picking apart Rousseau's First and Second Discourses. I have since learned that members are almost always very ordinary people, with very ordinary problems. Back then, I did not feel exceptionally bright. I had less than average grades in school. I knew my two best friends were both smarter than me.

Over two decades later, I had been married and was recently separated. I became interested in Mensa again. I felt that if I could gain entry into

Mensa, it would do my morale and self-image some good. I wrote away to them and received a self-administered home test. I did the test as honestly as I could. I sent them my answers and thought nothing more about it. A few weeks later I received a letter back. The general wording was something to the effect of "Dear Mr. Barsky: Thank you for your interest in our organization. We have evaluated your test. We find that your intelligence is well above the average of the population. However, our records show that four out of five individuals with your IQ failed to gain access to our organization. Thank you," et cetera.

For the next month, I felt that I had been put down. I mentioned this to one of my old friends, and he told me to look at it the other way.

"What does it mean if four out of five do not pass?"

My immediate response was "Then one out of five must pass."

"Damn right!"

"I'm gonna be the one."

A month later, I found myself taking the Mensa entrance exam. The supervisor was very good. He calmed me down. He explained that wrong answers would not count against me. It was a series of timed tests. When I was writing the third test, I noticed there was only 2 minutes to go. I was only two-thirds of the way through the test. My first reaction was to pick randomly B or C or D for the remaining series of questions. Probability dictated that I would have to get some of them right. But if I did that, and I passed, I would never know if I passed because I had the capacity or because I had spotted a loophole in the testing system. I had an image of myself making a classic blunder at one of the meetings, and everyone staring at me. "How did he get in here?" So I set out to complete the remaining questions, but I was only able to complete one or two more.

I passed! Since then, I have thought about it many times. Had I spent less time debating about randomly answering the remaining questions, would I have completed one or two more questions? This taught me about motivation. I had let myself become convinced that I could not get into Mensa. With just a little shove from a close friend, I accomplished my goal.

I wish that the children's story Dumbo the Flying Elephant had been optional reading for me during my teacher education program. Dumbo is a clumsy baby elephant in a circus. He has huge ears. He does not perform well as an elephant. He is put in a situation where he is stuck high up in the circus tent and told to fly. He doesn't believe he can. His trusted friends, the crows, tell him that if he holds onto this magic feather, he will be able to fly. With the help of his huge ears and this magic feather, Dumbo flies. Of course, there is no magic in the feather. It is just an ordinary feather. Dumbo believes he can do it, and he succeeds.

I believe that in teaching there is a large amount of power in self-fulfilling prophesies. When I tell my students they are smart and can perform, they do!

Learning from Students

My first practice teaching assignment was a marketing class, and I learned important lessons from students that I didn't even know I needed to learn.

My philosophy is to draw answers out of the students' mind. If students feel they "own" the answer, they are much more likely to remember it. I had the section on packaging to teach to grade 9 students. For homework, I asked them to go to a candy store and look at the different types of candy offered for sale. They were to pay attention to the packaging. I told them that in the next class, I would have every student stand up. They would not be allowed to sit down until each student had described a different form of packaging. For those students who simply took the school bus home and back, I asked them to research their memories. I thought this would be a fair and fun lesson assignment. The next day, I did what I told them I would do. The class stood up. I asked each student to give a different example of packaging as it applied to candy. I asked questions of the nongifted first so I would not embarrass a child. About one-third of the way, I asked a girl for her example. Her response was "I never get candy." I asked her what type of package did the candy have when her father gave her mother candy on a birthday or an anniversary. She replied, "We don't eat candy." I let her sit down.

My associate later told me that this girl was an ESL (English as a Second Language) student. Her parents had emigrated to Canada only a year ago. The girl probably only understood one word out of three that I said. She was telling the truth when she said she did not get candy.

The lesson I learned was the same one that the poet Robbie Burns had taught me: "The best laid schemes of mice and men gang aft awry." I had what I thought was a perfectly foolproof lesson plan. It was based on the assumption that all children eat candy. How does one anticipate a contingency like that? Today, I try to double-check my assumptions and develop a contingency plan, which I hope I never have to use.

A few days later, I was trying to illustrate "market research," the concept of knowing who and what comprises your target market. I used wrestling as an example because I thought it would be relevant to this class.

Years ago, back in the days of black and white TV, wrestlers wrestled. They did not act like thugs, hoodlums, actors, or comic book characters. There was a scientific air to the sport. The wrestlers entered the ring just wearing a bath robe. Maybe the robe had their name on the back, but that was all.

A company wanted to determine the major market segment of people who watched wrestling. They hired a market research company to do the study. When the results came back, they asked another company to do it, because they felt sure the first results were wrong. The results were the same. I asked the class if they could guess who the major market segment of the audience was that watched wrestling back in the early days. One girl waved her hand saying, "I know, I know." She said, "Older women?" When I said,

"You are right," she had a slip of the tongue and said, "I am?" I told the class that back in the early days (black and white TV) of wrestling, the main market segment that watched wrestling was women over 50.

This was the reason sporting events with predetermined outcomes became so popular in wrestling. To meet today's target market demands, today's wrestlers wear colorful costumes, strut and posture before a match, and wear makeup. They act like thugs and hoodlums (but don't tell them that to their face). One of my students yelled out, "They aren't all stupid. Some of them are pretty smart."

I replied, "I know that. Hulk Hogan used to be a banker."

The same student said, "One of them even is a chiropractor."

I looked at him and said, "They all are chiropractors!"

It was obvious that only a few students in the class knew what the word *chiropractor* meant. They started to giggle. Then other students started whispering to them, and they too, started to laugh. It only took about 30 seconds before the entire class was laughing.

I learned a lot from that one incident. It taught me something about the way students learn. Students do not need any motivation when they find learning fun. There were about 25 students who did not know what the word *chiropractor* implied. Most learned within 30 seconds. The class was willing to share with each other. Students who normally would not give each other the time of day were teaching the concept to each other.

Humor is a unique motivational tool in teaching. It is infectious, contagious, and soothing. I had the class's total attention for the rest of the period.

 ## Reflecting, Responding, and Writing

1. Describe what you have learned about teaching and learning from Gilbert's narrative. Explain how you can use the lessons learned in your teaching practice. Describe your plans to expand the range of sources from which you will draw for your professional learning.
2. Gilbert recognizes the value of his life experiences and personal relationships as sources of professional learning. Describe the significant learning you have done in the context of life's experiences and of personal relationships. Explain how this knowledge is relevant in the context of your current professional learning. Discuss your ideas with a colleague, listen carefully to his or her ideas, and reflect on what you hear. Document your reflections on the benefits of hearing from other prospective teachers regarding how they learn about becoming a teacher.

3. Gilbert describes a negative childhood experience, which he recalls was the most traumatic experience in his life at the time. In the context of becoming a teacher, he reviews it and learns from it. The event becomes "nutrition for creativity" and professional learning. Identify a negative childhood event that you can examine now from the perspective of the teacher you are becoming. Describe how you can relate to it differently from your current position and what you can learn from it. Reflect on the ways in which this new understanding could affect your work in classrooms and in schools. Document your reflections.

4. Gilbert's experiences in sports provide a rich resource for reflection and for learning about teaching. Identify a hobby or learning experience you have had in a nonacademic environment, and explore it for what it can teach you about teaching and learning. Identify a learning experience that involved mind-body coordination, such as learning to play a musical instrument, ski, or drive. Try to recall the learning processes as you experienced them. Relate your findings to your current teaching practices. Describe what these experiences have taught you about your current and future teaching.

5. Gilbert explores his experiences as a parent and describes what he has learned from children. Describe what you have learned from children in your roles as parent, friend, relative, or neighbor. Document these lessons. Reflect on the benefits of keeping in touch with children of all ages throughout your career in teaching. Describe how you plan to do this and document your ideas.

6. Invite a group of adolescents to your teacher education classroom to participate in a panel discussion about good teaching. Ask them to provide insights about the nature of good teaching and the kinds of teachers who help them to learn. Document the main ideas and relate them to your plans for professional development. Discuss these ideas with your colleagues, sharing insights, advice, and resources for ongoing learning.

7. The story of Dumbo provides a metaphor for believing in oneself and believing in students. It is a metaphor for believing that all things are possible when teachers and students learn to make their own meanings, and to live creative, responsive lives. Many fine examples of children's literature provide children with ways to imagine how things can be otherwise, to encourage them to question the givens, and to make new relations and new connections. *The Velveteen Rabbit* is one of

those stories; *Bridge to Terabithia* is another. Find your own examples, and share them with colleagues; they are as inspirational for prospective teachers as they are for children. Discuss these books in the context of the statement "Helping children to learn how to make relations is the central and most important task of pedagogy" (McDermott, 1986, p. 184). Organize a large-group discussion where you share ideas with colleagues about ways to help students to make connections and to see patterns, to investigate complex issues, and to engage in authentic inquiry. Organize a "book event" in which you and your colleagues share the lessons about teaching and learning you have gained from children's books.

8. Create a roundtable discussion group where you and your colleagues share your responses to Gilbert's narrative. Describe how you connect lessons learned in life to professional learning, and discuss ways to incorporate the ideas into your current and future professional practices. Document the main ideas that emerge from the discussion and your reflections on those ideas. Extending the ideas into practice, explore ways to help students to learn from life and from a wide variety of sources, to gain self-knowledge, and to enjoy the critical and creative processes of genuine inquiry.

CHAPTER 8

Creating Relationships: Learning *from* and *with* Students in the Classroom

The arts are among the resources through which individuals re-create themselves. The work *of art is a process that culminates in a new art form. That art form is the re-creation of the individual.*

ELLIOT EISNER

Ellen Shifrin's narrative of professional learning focuses on learning *from* and *with* students. She emphasizes the creation of shared understandings, shared meanings, and shared values in classroom settings. Ellen explores the metaphor of "teaching as like being in a good relationship." She describes her understanding of the teaching-learning relationship as one that enables students to be actively engaged in their own learning and inquiry. She deals with her ongoing and persistent efforts to establish intimate and caring relationships with large numbers of high school students, and to make classroom learning relevant, meaningful, and enjoyable for them.

Ellen's narrative describes the components of good relationships, and the value and relevance of good relationships in enhancing the quality of students' experiences in classrooms and in schools. She describes the dynamics of being responsive to students, of sharing responsibility, and of cooperating with students in the design and enactment of curriculum. She also describes the difficulties and realities of working in this way with students—of encouraging them to make connections between their minds and bodies, of freeing themselves to express their inner emotional lives, of challenging themselves intellectually, and of engaging in an ongoing inquiry—when they are not accustomed to doing so. Permeating her practices is her abiding belief in the importance of openness, honesty, respect, and trust between teachers and students. Her narrative describes the movement from "connection with the self" to "connection with others" to "connection toward shared meaning making and understanding." It provides insights into one prospective teacher's efforts to be sensitive and responsive to students in high school settings, to learn from and with them, and to teach in a way that "provides ongoing stimulation, excitement, and challenges" for both teacher and students.

Learning to Teach: Moving beyond Power, Control, and Manipulation

by Ellen Shifrin

But the power, the manipulation, the control—all these are ways of operating that I really want to get away from. I don't want to have control, to be the "top banana," to manipulate students and material and myself in such a way to convince anyone that it is valuable and even interesting and enriching to do this or that, to push my way of being on anyone else.

(Professional Journal, 1991)

After almost 8 months at the faculty of education, I was still in limbo, trying to decide where to go, whether I even wanted to remain a teacher. From time to time I considered becoming something else, but I have been a teacher of one sort or another for 20 years. So it was only with great difficulty that I even imagined doing something else. But there are aspects of teaching that bother me, one in particular. The following story and reflections from my practice teaching journal illustrate my struggle with the issues of power and control.

At one point during the second week I had one of the Gatsby classes read and write in their reading logs for about 10 or 15 minutes. . . . All but two of the students were doing it; the room was generally quiet. But a couple of students were still horsing around, talking, clearly not doing as everyone else was. And that can be disruptive not only to me but also to the rest of the class. So I went over and asked the fellow who was turned around talking to turn around, face his own desk, and start doing the work, to take advantage of the time to read a bit. He did it. I felt really weird about doing that, though. The power of it felt most uncomfortable. I said something; he did it, with some reluctance. I had to work a little harder with him than with most of the class, but nevertheless he bowed to my superior place in this system.

Another incident occurred later in the week. . . . One of the girls, who might have been away for the first class that I taught, expressed the opinion that she did not like to interrupt her reading with writing down "first thoughts" in a response journal. We talked about it a bit, and I tried to explain to her, obviously not successfully, about the process, its flexibility, its purpose. Finally, I said that just because she had never done this before doesn't mean that it's not an accepted practice, that it has been a proven way of increasing appreciation for a book, and that many teachers use this regularly. Reluctantly, she stopped questioning.

(Professional Journal, 1991)

The issues of power, control, and manipulation have been a concern for some time. My teaching strategy in a college theater program where I have taught for 9 years was about how to manipulate the material so that the students would enjoy it and have fun learning it. The realization that I had completely and unconsciously fallen into the trap of manipulating was brought home during an improvisation class I took one year in order to better appreciate what my students were learning. I have drawn from my personal journal an excerpt that illustrates this realization.

Last Sunday [the teacher was telling a student] that his ideas were just as good as anyone else's ideas. . . . I remembered that, because, of course, I need that kind of feedback also. So I was quite insistent this past Sunday that people were going to follow my ideas. But then the feedback I got was that I wasn't listening to those I was working with, that I was forcing them to do what I wanted to do. In other words, I was being manipulative (my word). This was depressing and somewhat horrifying. But I have been thinking about it quite a bit, and I've come up with what I think is either a rationalization or an explanation: In teaching and parenting, two occupations with which I am totally entwined, one is always getting others to do what one wants them to do, one is always teaching, trying to get people to behave in a certain way, to surprise them into learning this material by manipulating the situation so that they do learn in spite of themselves. I've spent a lot of time trying to get that technique down. . . . But this doesn't work in an improv class because I'm not teaching anyone anything. I'm supposed to be relating to people and trying to interact spontaneously. . . . But the thing about being manipulative really bothered me, because of course I don't like to think of myself as being manipulative. Who does? It'll be something to think about and watch for during the next year as I learn more about teaching.

(Professional Journal, 1990)

In that passage I am genuinely taken aback by the realization that what I have been engaging in is manipulation. Over the course of my year in formal teacher education, I came to accept that manipulation can be used to positive effect. If one believes that younger people require some assistance, some guidance toward learning about and understanding the world and making decisions about their own situation in it, then our task as teachers is to provide them with the stimuli and the environment that will aid in achieving this end. But our role seems to become muddy in the doing. Power, in its negative sense (domination over, without due consideration for others) rears its unappealing head. For many students, the bottom line is that in the end, the teachers give grades; a power more awesome is hard to picture. Not only do the helpless students have to try to please the teachers, but they also have to figure out what pleases whom, since teachers have a wide variety of standards. There are many stories of students who cease working in a particular class because they learn that their effort does not govern their grade.

Good Teaching: Good Relationship

I am on the "side" of the student, probably because I have never ceased being one. Throughout my life I have returned to the classroom or studio to learn from other teachers. How can one possibly consider entering the "system" when one feels more like a "growing-up" than a "grown-up"? The answer is, of course, one cannot. Can one even be a teacher at all? I look to my ideals to begin to answer that question.

Consider the following simile:

Good teaching is like being in a good relationship. It is stimulating, one-on-one, caring, full of trust, fun, the process is as important as the goal, honesty, sharing, exploring, cooperation, taking responsibility, moving with others, mind-body connection, going into depth, letting go, accepting, meaningful, gentle.

Some of these aspects of teaching existed already in my teaching. Some of them were (and are) still not developed. To define where I was as a teacher and where I was headed, I will explore this image through definitions, stories, and reflections.

Summerhill: **A Learning Experience Story**

Less than a year after I finished high school, I decided to try the university again. . . . In April I gave notice to my employer . . . and set to work in order to regain entry into the university. Accomplishing this necessitated rewriting three matriculation exams to elevate my score from 670-odd to a minimum of 700. I passionately hated high school, so this was no easy chore.

My parents, thrilled that I wanted to study, hired a cousin to tutor me. He was several years older and had performed extremely well in school. He was the logical person to attempt the challenge of working with me.

We set up a card table desk in the basement. . . . The season was spring, a long-awaited event, so it was doubly difficult to keep mind to task. . . . For 6 weeks my cousin came to tutor me, three times a week. We sat at the card table and plowed our way through the necessary texts.

It turned out that my cousin was smart not only in school but also in "real life." Today he is a psychologist. His future orientation became crystal clear to me through his first act in the tutoring process: he gave me a copy of *Summerhill* [Neill, 1960] to read. I read about this progressive school that was based on the principles of freedom, creativity, responsibility, and self-determination and had been founded in England in 1921. My life changed. I was totally enthralled. Education could be like this? Not forced, not stupid, not only about what the adults wanted? Here was a whole new world indeed.

I thought about the Summerhill school a great deal that spring. My cousin and I discussed it every time we met. Summerhill served to establish some baseline ideas about education for me. It acted as a guiding light, a source of inspiration, as I plodded away studying pieces of information I considered unbearably dull and useless.

At Summerhill adults shared power with students. They allowed kids to find their own way, rather than shoving accepted norms down gagging throats. This school seemed to be based on a philosophy of caring, of listening to each unique person, of treating each student and teacher as though they genuinely mattered. Because many "problem" kids wound up at Summerhill, the adults were required to possess huge quantities of patience. The goal here was not to turn out good grades but to help all students find a path on which they might begin their travels in life, a way to happiness in its fullest sense. Summerhill was my first view of a possible utopia.

As my cousin and I strove toward better marks, underneath it all my imagination was kindled by other potentialities. Studying Summerhill raised the whole "cramming" process to a level of noninvolvement in the means to attain a desired end.

(Professional Journal, 1991)

Defining Relationships in the Classroom

One-on-one: one teacher, one learner, both of whom are also doing the other activity; that is, the teacher is learning and the learner is teaching (my definition).

In a one-on-one approach, the teacher and the learner can both ask, answer, discuss, lead, and follow, in a fully engaged way. The teacher, in the "mature" role, finds what will engage the learner. The learner's task is to understand and respond so that the learner is satisfied and/or challenged. It is not my intention to elaborate on techniques for accomplishing this, but it seems that, in many cases, a one-on-one situation is the most intensive way to learn. In the "Summerhill" story, we see a disinterested learner becoming enthusiastic and engaged as a result of a teacher who finds a way in.

The next excerpt from my practice teaching journal documents one such opportunity for this kind of teaching in one of my practice teaching sessions.

> One of the students was quite upset with a grade I had given her on the reading response journal. She had misunderstood what I had asked them to do. Now this is a smart girl who knows how to play the game, and she is clearly interested in doing the right thing to get good marks. I explained to her that at this point there was nothing I could do, since I was leaving and there was no time to redo and remark. I also said that if I was going to be here longer, I would give her an opportunity to hand it in again, now that she understands what was expected, that I would have worked with her more so that we might have understood each other better.

> (Professional Journal, 1991)

That moment of one-on-one interaction was invigorating and full of lessons. Care and caring relations is another part of the good teaching/good relationship analogy. If teachers really care, students can accept their teachers' imperfections with (some) equanimity.

> *Striving always to see the learning event from the standpoint of the student, the teacher teaches by actively pursuing the student's objective, an objective that teacher and student have together constructed. In a caring relation, the student responds by engaging fully in the event. He or she grows, and the teacher seeing this knows that teaching has had a desirable effect.*

> i.e. Witherall and Noddings, 1991, p. 7

Trust is another essential quality in the teacher-student relationship, and I have drawn from my professional journal to reflect on this quality here. After the fiasco with my first grade 12 class, I chatted with the teacher who asked me what my thoughts were on reasons why the imagining exercise I had used hadn't worked. I said that it hadn't worked because (a) the students and I hadn't built up a relationship yet and so they didn't really trust me, and (b) they hadn't been doing that kind of thing all year, so it was strange and perhaps scary for them. She agreed with me.

> Yesterday morning I woke up with some thoughts about trust: Little babies trust everyone. As we grow we learn not to trust. Then we have to learn to trust some individuals, and as individuals we have to earn someone's trust. We have to prove ourselves trustworthy. As teachers we should be trustworthy. But most high school students do not trust their

teachers. They have learned during the course of their school lives that many teachers are not to be trusted. So it is quite an uphill battle to gain the trust of students. It seems somehow so perverted to have to prove oneself worthy of being trusted. In an ideal society, everyone would trust everyone else. In fact, it wouldn't be an issue at all; the word *trust* probably wouldn't even exist.

(Professional Journal, 1991)

Now I take care to build trust and not to expect it too soon from the new students. Their first year is a time to become acquainted, to get used to taking risks, not to be "thrown to the lions," so to speak.

Exploring Situations in the Classroom

Good teacher-student relationships provide the context for explorations in learning. Exploration requires an openness, a willingness to listen to others, and a release from expectations. Exploration requires trust, and I have explored my own understandings of the connection by reflecting on a practical situation in a classroom. I have drawn the following excerpt from my professional journal:

> Not knowing exactly what to do, I organized the class into two groups: those who wanted to try to solve the mystery of the missing lighter and those who wanted to continue with the class work. . . . I did not know what steps to take. . . . Clearly I had to discard the lesson plan and attend fully to this issue. We all sat in a circle, and I asked each in turn to say whatever was on their minds about this dilemma. Most of the students couldn't believe that someone had actually stolen the lighter. I myself felt that indeed someone had taken it, but I was surprised that it hadn't shown up. One student tried to rationalize—perhaps someone had unconsciously put it in their backpack! Most expressed disappointment. One student said he felt he couldn't trust anyone in the class anymore. Others said that because this was drama class, they had a special relationship, with trust as an important aspect; now this was at least partially destroyed.

> When everyone had spoken, the dilemma still felt unresolved; it was not yet time to return to the lesson plan. I asked how many people had been robbed. Several students put up their hands, and so we heard theft stories for the rest of the period.

> What did I learn? I relearned that the teacher can ask the students what to do. They'll generate lots of ideas. I learned that even though I didn't know what to do, I still did something: I listened, and when I was ready, I made my own suggestions (sitting in the circle and the activities that followed). I learned that I had to go with trusting the students in spite of the fact that I wasn't sure if they were putting me on. Even if the whole

stolen lighter event was a hoax, we still shared some good storytelling.
I learned that these students were capable and willing to offer alternative
solutions, given the opportunity.

(Professional Journal, 1991)

This entry exemplifies a number of the qualities I have sought in my development as a teacher. It emphasizes trust, caring (about finding the truth), and
letting go of the original goal, which leads to the process being as important
as the goal. It highlights the importance of sharing, cooperating, exploring,
and taking responsibility for one's own learning. As a teacher, I encourage
students to assume responsibility for themselves, although I am often met with
great resistance. It is always a joy when students do so or when they seem to
have this capability naturally.

In the following "Teaching *Romeo and Juliet*" story from my professional
journal, the responsibility story is embedded in the larger context. I include
parts of it here because it also illustrates a spirit of cooperation, sharing, honesty, and the importance and honoring of process. As a teaching-learning
experience, it is one of my fondest memories.

Teaching *Romeo and Juliet*

We began the dance course with the Renaissance era, at the beginning
of the 17th century. As this coincides with Shakespeare's era, I decided
to place the dances in the context of one or more of his plays. Two plays
contain the instruction to dance; *Romeo and Juliet* is one of them.

First I taught the dances—galliards, pavans, branles, almans; we
even tackled the lavolta, a dance where the man lifts his partner up in the
air as they both turn three-quarters around. We shared much laughter in
the attempt to master this one. As the students became proficient at the
dances, we turned to the script. The ballroom scene from *Romeo and
Juliet* where the two lovers first meet and kiss includes dancing.

As soon as the rehearsal schedule was set, I suddenly realized that
I had absolutely no idea how to direct a scene. But with the students'
help—they were taking a directing course—we managed to make
Shakespeare's words live and to maneuver the actors around the stage.
Since the raison d'être was to show off the students' skill in historical
movement and dance, we kept everything else simple.

As time progressed, the students were doing so well that we decided
to give a studio performance. About a month before performance date,
we had to schedule extra rehearsals. The only time available to all was
eight o'clock in the morning! We arrived bleary-eyed with large
Styrofoam cups of coffee, but once in the studio we worked hard. By
9:30, when regular classes began, we had accomplished a lot.

One morning one student took a taxi; another student learned about
tact and responsibility; we all learned about cooperation, giving, and

receiving and about depending on one another. The performance was a great success. As a teaching-learning experience it is one of my fondest memories. A spirit of cooperation guided us all as we worked toward the goal of presentation.

(Professional Journal, 1986–1987)

Cooperation, Sharing, Process, and Honesty

More recently, one of my practice teaching experiences also included all of these elements: cooperation, sharing, process, and honesty. Although the subject matter and mode of teaching are different, the unifying factor is that I did not know something: in the "Teaching *Romeo and Juliet*" story, I did not know how to direct; in the next story, I did not "own" the material.

The Judith Thompson Seminar

Today I presented the Judith Thompson seminar to the English OAC [Ontario Academic Credit] class. We read and discussed a few scenes from the play, and then I handed out some short articles for them to read, with students getting different ones, so that everyone could contribute something to the discussion. They read silently and made notes for 15 minutes. A short break, then on to discussion of the articles, which happened quite spontaneously, and then on to a final 20 minutes of a cold reading of the play, which was punctuated by lots of talking. Needless to say, we didn't get through all the scenes I had planned. The reading ended with one of the monologues; it was extremely well read by one of the students, and we were all quite moved.

The teacher and I had discussed my anxiety about the Thompson material because I do not "own" the material yet. We talked about the benefits of various forms of presentation, and she mentioned a teacher who had developed a cooperative structure because of some particular weaknesses. So not owning the material and having a rather undynamic lecture style can become a strength: by necessity the students engage in their own learning; instead of lecturing, the teacher creates the environment where learning occurs together and responsibility is shared.

(Professional Journal, 1991)

Frankly, the Judith Thompson seminar would have fallen flat on its face had the students not agreed to cooperate, to engage themselves in the discussion, silent reading, and play reading. I was completely dependent on their cooperation. Perhaps because the seminar took place during my second week at the school, they were willing; to some extent I had gained their trust and respect. This seminar was about process; students had no goal other than to learn something about Judith Thompson: no exam, no essay, no evaluation of any kind. We were simply a group of people sitting around a table, learning, exploring together. We learned from and with each other.

Teaching in Depth

Going into depth is an aspect of the good teaching/good relationship analogy that has retained its significance for me over the years. Generally there is a choice between "covering the material" or looking in detail in all my teaching experiences. In my classes at the college, I have opted for greater understanding of a smaller amount, but in secondary school where one must meet outside guidelines, there is little time for qualitative exploration.

It is very frustrating to try to teach something without enough time. . . . I am feeling that I would be frustrated by the whole system—always flitting over the material instead of being allowed to stay with something and look at it from a variety of perspectives.

(Professional Journal, 1990)

I believe that in-depth work is part of my makeup as a person because of my training as a dancer, as a dance historian, and as a movement analyst. In teaching I always aim to balance between an exploration that satisfies me and one that will not discourage students accustomed to a superficial approach. Work that is in-depth is full of meaning for me. In my drama and English classes we spent some time discussing how classes might be made more meaningful for the students we teach. I learned ways to present the material, the class content, so that it would be worthwhile to the students. I draw from my professional journal to show how meaningful this is to me in my teaching. I know I am making a difference in their lives.

These two classes stand out because I felt as though I had really accomplished something with the students. In the first, once I had read the writing I was totally impressed with their ability to express their emotional life. They had obviously connected with the visualization we had done. So I felt like I had made a difference, that I had something to offer them, that I could create a situation so that they had a . . . meaningful experience.

(Professional Journal, 1990)

Care, Sensitivity, Gentleness, and Fun

In a much earlier camp teaching experience in 1965, I had somehow created a significant experience for a child, but at the time I didn't know how or why. I wrote this story because the event was significant and because it informs my current professional practice.

One day I learned that they are sending me a girl I'll call Andrea, who has been the camp problem. Andrea had been coming to overnight camp since she was about 5! She gives everyone a hard time. I am nervous about having her in the class.

To everyone's amazement, she responds beautifully to the discipline of ballet. She is only briefly difficult in class and now settles in to master the basics. I am probably giving them a class that is slightly beyond them, because that way the kids get to do turns, and this is working well. They come; they are more or less on time. They work hard. . . . And Andrea is becoming increasingly pleasant elsewhere, too. The staff and the camp director are pleased.

Why should this work? A camp counselor, a camper who doesn't want to be at camp, a ballet class. Presto, everyone's happy. . . . I don't know what I did to make Andrea happy. Maybe it was the little bit of added positive attention given to her. Perhaps it was the discipline that Andrea responded to. Or maybe she enjoyed moving her body in a rhythmic, structured way. . . . There was satisfaction in reaching a difficult child.

(Professional Journal, 1965)

Gentleness is a quality I value highly. Human beings should be treated with sensitivity and care. My associate teachers thought that my gentleness with the students was almost always appropriate, and one associate teacher said:

Although Ellen has a fairly quiet speaking voice, there is a calmness to it . . . very gentle with the students, almost too gentle. . . . Her speech is clear, measured, and gentle. Students respond attentively to her quiet confidence. . . . Personal response was warm, sensitive. Easy-going manner. Doesn't force the answers—allows "space" for students. . . . She was sensitive to their level of expertise.

(Associate Teacher's Evaluation Report, 1991)

Fun, the quality that hopefully needs no definition, emerges over and over again in all the stories I have written.

So I'm always looking for ways to get them to learn in a pleasant and enjoyable way so that they don't even experience the learning as learning. . . . I believe she also uttered an exasperated cry, something like "arrrrghhh!". . . Even though I started them off on what I thought was a somewhat high note—doing a warmup to Janet Jackson . . . I had to laugh about it, though. . . . We were playing "this is a hat." . . . We shared much laughter in the attempt to master this one. . . . I am probably giving them a class that is slightly beyond them, because that way the kids get to do turns, and this is working well.

(Professional Journal, 1991)

My work in schools has always been geared toward making learning enjoyable, even in the study of depressing classics such as *Death of a Salesman* and *The Great Gatsby*. An associate said of me, "She made the classes fun. Her enthusiasm for what she was teaching spilled over and, as a result, the students were into it" (Associate Teacher's Evaluation Report, 1991).

I am more comfortable in my discomfort about teaching in high schools. I continue to explore; I take more risks now than I ever did. Nothing is ever the same, and this provides ongoing stimulation, excitement, and challenges.

Lessons to Live By

- Take your work 100% seriously. You are working with human beings.
- Always strive to uncover the truth.
- Place yourself in the student role at least once a year.
- Maintain your integrity.
- Question your motivation for everything.
- Communicate with other teachers.
- Have the courage to face what is true, especially if you are not enjoying yourself.
- Think about what's *really* important at least once a day.
- Learn *from* and *with* your students.

 Reflecting, Responding, and Writing

1. Describe the role that Ellen plays in teacher-student relationships. Describe your understanding of "care" and "caring relations" in the context of your role as teacher. Share your ideas with a colleague. Discuss differences and similarities in your understandings. Reflect on the discussion, and document your reflections. Organize a classroom symposium on the topic of "Care and Caring Relations" in classrooms and schools. Discuss the nature, the dimensions, and the boundaries of care in professional relationships. Consider the difficulties of care when others are unpleasant, disrespectful, and uncaring. Share ideas, strategies, and suggestions in this large group setting where you can learn from a wide range of perspectives, levels of expertise, and richness of background experience.

2. Ellen uses the simile "Good teaching is like being in a good relationship." How do you respond to this simile? Explain how it relates to your teaching. Find a simile that works for

you, and describe its qualities and components in the context of teaching.

3. Ellen describes her less-than-successful attempts to enact her belief in the mind-body connection in a grade 10 classroom with inexperienced students. Identify a situation in your own past practices where you have tried to enact a personal value, principle, or theory that was not successful in the practical situation. What did you do about the situation at the time? How did you subsequently reconcile the value/principle/theory and the practice in the context of your professional practice?

4. Ellen begins her narrative by identifying her struggle with the power-and-control aspect of teaching. How do you deal with this issue in your classroom practice? Describe how you create relationships with students so that they understand their responsibilities within those relationships and abide by them. Discuss your ideas with a colleague. Organize a large-group discussion around this issue where you can avail of the ideas, perspectives, and strategies of others. Document the discussion.

5. At the end of Ellen's narrative, she expresses her pleasure with the associate teacher's recognition of her gentleness, quiet confidence, and sensitivity toward students—as these are qualities she values in herself. Describe the qualities you value in yourself as a teacher and the ways in which you pay attention to preserving and developing these qualities on an ongoing basis, even in the face of obstacles and difficulties.

6. Create a small-group setting with colleagues to discuss Ellen's narrative, to reflect together on the ways she uses what she knows to learn about teaching high school students, and to explore the ways you can learn from her narrative of professional learning.

7. Ellen's narrative provides insights into the movement from "connection with the self" to "connection with others" to "connection toward shared meaning making and understanding" in the context of professional learning. McIntyre (1998) explains that the ability to "learn with others by co-creating something together—new knowledge, new understanding, new perspective" (p. 35), is the highest form of relational learning. Reflect on your personal experiences in each of the three phases of relational learning in the context of your current work with students in classrooms. Discuss your ideas with a small group of colleagues. Giving examples from your classroom practices, share ideas, things that have worked for

you, and experiences that have been less than successful! Document the main ideas of the discussion. Using the three-phase model, design a plan for your professional development as a learner-in-relation and as a teacher-in-relation, a professional who

- learns *about self* through interactions with others;
- learns *about others* and exchanges information, ideas, and understandings with others, and
- learns *with others* by co-creating meanings, understandings, perspectives, and values together.

8. Ellen challenges the mind-body relationship enacted in most classrooms and schools. She suggests a greater emphasis on the education of the senses and respect for the body's ways of knowing in the education of adolescents. Work with a small group of your colleagues to discuss the ways you could incorporate Ellen's ideas and strategies into your teaching. Discuss the ways in which this way of teaching could enhance students' learning. Exchange stories and anecdotes of your own learning through the senses and of times when you have entered into a learning experience through one of the senses. Discuss ways to help students to overcome obstacles to learning by making connections to their senses of sound, sight, touch, and taste in a classroom setting. Document the discussion, and reflect on the ways in which you will incorporate your understandings of the mind-body connection into curriculum design, teaching strategies, and assessment methods.

CHAPTER 9

The Community in the Classroom

We are freed when we begin to put justice, heartfelt relationships and the service of others and of truth over and above our own needs for love, success, or our fears of failure.

JEAN VANIER

Alicia Cashore's narrative describes the circles of meaning making created by one prospective teacher as she continually connects her growing awarenesses and new understandings with her classroom practices. Her account of professional learning highlights the ways in which theory and practice support and enrich each other, enabling her to transform her understandings and practices. Alicia shows how collaborative inquiry, reflection, and continuous feedback from others enabled her to adapt and enrich her curriculum and teaching strategies, and to be increasingly more responsive to her students. In this account of her professional learning, she uses a framework of practice teaching episodes to describe how she learned by doing, reflecting, and talking about what she had done and by responding to feedback from associate teachers, her team-teaching colleague, and students. She explains how she came to understand teaching as a "team effort, not as an individual one." She presents a portrait of a beginning teacher who is self-consciously reflective about what she thinks and does. She is collaborative, collegial, and willing and able to learn from and with others.

Alicia's account of professional learning presents an alternative to those accounts of becoming a teacher that show beginning teachers "in survival mode," focused on the mechanics of teaching and unable to deal with the complexities of life in classrooms and schools. Her narrative also challenges the traditional image of teachers as solitary individuals working behind closed doors, intent on teaching the content of their subject disciplines and oblivious to the people with whom they are interacting. It tells of how she challenged that image and changed her understanding of the teacher's role from one who teaches science to one who teaches students. Alicia also explains how she transformed her understanding of professional learning from that which is solitary and individualistic to that which is collegial and collaborative. She shows how she willingly engages in team planning with colleagues because of the opportunity to "share experience, expertise, and ideas and to learn from others." Her narrative illustrates the interplay of practice and theory in her daily life as a teacher, and the ways in which she makes continuous connections between them through reflection and inquiry.

Becoming a Teacher: Snapshots from the Photo Album

by Alicia Cashore

There are four pivotal snapshots that I think show my professional growth, defining the teacher that I am and illustrating the journey I have taken to get here. I can trace a significant portion of the journey by looking at my four practice teaching sessions, and I will use those four snapshots to tell my story.

Learning to be a teacher in a year was an intense experience; the personal growth and development involved exceeded anything I had anticipated. Looking back, my memories from this year appear as snapshots in a photo album. Several snapshots near the front of the album show who I was at the beginning of the year. I arrived with a master's degree in biology and four years' experience as a teaching assistant, excited at the prospect of being a science teacher. My main focus through the year was going to be the science curriculum. By contrast, the most recent snapshots show a teacher focused on so much more than content and committed to teaching students rather than teaching science. Many of those snapshots in the middle show classes, workshops, discussions, and readings—the classroom management workshop, the employment conference, and the hours spent in reflection and inquiry.

Making a Start

The first snapshot is a bit fuzzy and unfocused. There are uncertainties and insecurities; the dominant features seem to be questions and anxiety. Although it was only 6 months ago, as I write this, the teacher in the photo seems very young.

Practice Teaching, Session One (PT1), seems like a lifetime ago. Despite my previous teaching experience I was feeling very green. In the first 2 months of methods classes, the focus had been on specific techniques for teaching science, using spectacular demonstrations or "magic tricks." I thought that the use of such magic tricks was the norm at every high school, which was an extremely intimidating prospect. I walked into my first placement focused entirely on the actual tricks I could use, unable to focus on the kind of teacher I already was and on the kind of teacher I wanted to become.

One of my most important insights during PT1 was that the magic tricks were not the norm. There was no quick and easy way to help students to understand the concepts being taught. Good teachers worked hard to explain the concepts and to guide the students' understanding, directing their inquiry and seizing any interesting facts or examples to inspire their interest.

Throughout PT1, I learned several lessons. From my associate, I learned about lesson organization. He spent the first 5 minutes reviewing the day's agenda with the students. On my second day, I was so nervous that I forgot to do this, and I noticed a difference in the students' focus. It helped the students to know what they were doing in class, which in turn, made my job easier. I learned to tune in to the level of understanding and the needs of the students. I was teaching an advanced biology class, for which I had to adjust my pace repeatedly. I started off too slowly, then overcompensated and moved too quickly, without giving the students enough direction. Finding the right pace required interaction with the students to gauge their understanding. I also learned the value of knowing the students' names. It took me a week to learn all the names, but when I was able to address most of the students by name, they paid much more attention to me and seemed to try harder.

During PT1, I began to be aware of the multiculturalism issue. One of the aspects of the school that I noticed immediately was the huge cultural diversity of the students; more than 70 countries were represented within the student population. Less than 5% of the student body was white, a trend that was not reflected in the teacher population. In fact, with the teachers, it was the opposite.

Throughout the 2 weeks I used a variety of lesson plan formats to see what worked best for me. I discovered that there is no substitute for content knowledge. As long as I knew the day's objectives and was comfortable with the content, the format made no difference. In fact, when I was comfortable with the content, I tended not to need my lesson plans. I was focused on learning to do basic things.

If I had to summarize what I learned in PT1, it would be the mechanics of teaching: managing the workload, knowing students' names, running a class, shaping a lesson. It was a start. However, I still wasn't focused on my professional self. I still wasn't defining my teacher self.

Tuning In to Students and Feeling Like a Teacher

The next snapshot is clearer than the first. There is still anxiety, especially because the subject in this teaching session is an unfamiliar one. But the image is stronger, better defined and more in control. The teacher in the photo looks as if she's enjoying the experience, not simply surviving it.

My second placement followed right on the heels of PT1, starting only 2 weeks later. I was teaching chemistry, a subject with which I was not completely comfortable. Ironically, I found it easier to teach. By the time I had reviewed the content enough to be able to teach it, I had significantly reduced my preparation for the next 2 weeks. In Practice Teaching Two (PT2), I started to shape my teaching and focus on more than the content. Specifically, I wanted the students to be able to apply their knowledge, to develop their analytical skills. I kept those objectives in mind as I prepared for each lesson.

The first class I taught during PT2 was typical of my entire experience there. Although I was still nervous, the lesson on trends in the periodic table went well. I gave the students time to copy the information about each trend from the overhead; then I used a question-and-answer format to test their understanding before I continued. All the students were engaged; I could see the proverbial light bulbs going on as they connected with what I was saying. Most students were eager to answer my questions; many started anticipating the next connection before I explained it. It was very exciting for me to see their comprehension.

There was also an element of comic relief, which I think made everyone relax, including me. The overhead and the periodic table were on opposite sides of the room, and very little space was available for me to walk from one to the other. Every time I did, I tripped on the trash can, until I moved it. I also kept dropping the meter stick I was using as a pointer. But at the end of one class, a student said to me, "That was a good lesson." Another said, "You weren't as nervous as the last student teacher." Their comments were very gratifying.

What was the basis for this positive experience? I was prepared and could help the students to connect with the content. I was confident with the material, which gave the students confidence in me and helped to give me the confidence to teach. I kept student involvement high by using the question-and-answer technique, but I also gave them time to copy out the notes, so that they had something to use as a basis for participating as we applied each concept. I think I communicated well with them, and I was enthusiastic. The students were also well prepared, in that my associate had taught them the background they needed to understand the periodic table. I can't take credit for that support, but I can certainly learn from it.

Multiculturalism was central again in this experience. This was another school with a very mixed student population. Fewer nationalities were represented than in the first school, but the percentage was similar in terms of the

racial and cultural minorities representing about 95% of the student population. And again, the cultural diversity of the student population was not
reflected among the teachers.

In addition, during this placement, a horrifying racial incident occurred at
another school, where several nonwhite teachers were threatened and one
was assaulted. This incident focused my attention even more on the issue of
multiculturalism in schools. Among other things, I realized it could not have
happened at the schools where I was teaching, because of their culturally
diverse population.

In terms of my professional development, PT2 was significant to my professional learning. I started to relax, I developed a lot more confidence, and I really
started to feel like a teacher. I was starting to define my style in terms of my
teaching personality, the kind of rapport I could develop with the students, and
the kind of emphasis I wanted to put on the content. I was also focusing more on
what I think is an extremely important issue in teaching. I was learning more
about the role and status of multiculturalism in the schools, defining my opinion
more clearly, and relating all this to my classroom practices.

Cumulative Threads: Adapting to the Real World

In the next snapshot, the focus is getting clearer and clearer. Other changes
have occurred as well. The uncertainty is gone, the anxiety is diminishing.
Questions remain, but they have changed. They deal less with the general
processes of teaching and more with specific issues and situations. The
teacher in the snapshot is looking more relaxed and confident.

Practice Teaching Three (PT3) was probably where I grew the most.
I was team-teaching with another student teacher, which gave me some
huge insights into this profession. I was dealing with general-level classes
and lower grade levels, which really forced me to define my approach.
I also saw a variety of different teaching styles, and I was able to see in
them a lot of what I do or what I want to do in my own teaching.

Team teaching was a valuable exercise in compromise and cooperation
for 2 weeks. My coteacher liked to incorporate activities into each lesson,
which I had not done before but which worked very well. We had some ram-
bunctious kids in every class. The activities gave them a chance to work off
their excess energy, improving their focus and concentration for the rest of
each lesson.

My associate was very good at "reading" a class, figuring out what students might need in terms of motivation or direction and adjusting her lesson
accordingly. She had some very valuable advice about how to deal with difficult students. Probably the most important was that the teacher had to establish control at the beginning of the year, or the class could be lost. This
associate had a different teaching style than my previous associates.

Basically, she presented the content in overlapping threads, tying everything together as she went along and always including relevant examples. My other associates tended to teach in blocks, one or two concepts each day, focusing on that block rather than how it fit in to the whole unit. Toward the end of the unit, it would theoretically become clear how everything fit together.

I see advantages and disadvantages to both methods. I think students need some information in blocks, particularly in math and science. The structure helps them to focus on the content, to have a snapshot of that concept. Also, science is a very structured subject, so by giving structure to the content, the teacher models how to do science. That being said, I also feel that each concept needs to be given context within the unit and within the real world. I'm not sure the students, especially general level kids, can fit the concepts together on their own.

I think the ideal model is a combination of the two, in which the concepts are introduced as blocks, but with trailing threads. These threads would be woven into future blocks, with all the threads being cumulative, so the content would be given context relative to the rest of the unit. Simply put, it means referring to previous (and, if appropriate, to future) concepts, so the students get the big picture while still having some structure. I think this approach teaches students to bring their existing knowledge to new situations, to be able to combine several concepts and apply them. It teaches them to trust their knowledge, to rely on it, and to be able to use it.

In terms of my professional development, then, PT3 had a major impact. Through this experience I was able to define how I would structure a unit, to develop a sense of how important it is to give context and relevance to the content, and to bring that relevance to a topic. I also got a sense of teaching as a team effort, not an individual effort. This goes beyond the formalities of team teaching: a solo teacher is a member of a department and of a school staff. In addition to classroom responsibilities, each teacher brings certain expertise and opinions and ideas to the team and, at the same time, learns from the rest of the team.

Learning to Be Adaptable: Adapting to the Learner

The final snapshot is the clearest and best focused so far. The situation is actually very different from the first three, because it is at an adult high school. But the teacher in this last snapshot has the confidence to adapt to adult students and the ability to anticipate and deal with the unique challenges of teaching a high school curriculum to adults. In this snapshot, the teacher has a very realistic perspective on her role and is enjoying the full experience.

My last placement was a perfect ending to the various practice teaching experiences I had during the year. I had a mixed bag of classes; for 2 1/2 weeks, I taught biology, chemistry, and English as a Second Language (ESL) science. In an earlier placement, that schedule would have made me quit. But at the end of the year I was happy to have it.

In Practice Teaching Four (PT4), I developed several specific teaching skills. I really had to adjust the pace of my lessons for the students. The adults asked more questions than adolescents, so I was rarely able to cover all the content in a given lesson. I had to adjust to the students in another way that may be unique to adults. Although my morning class started at 9:00, I rarely had a full class until 9:30. If they had been adolescents, I would have made it their responsibility to get the notes they missed in the first half hour. But the adults who were late had very valid reasons. Many of them worked late every night, and many of them had family commitments that made it impossible to arrive any earlier. So I had to adjust my lesson plans so they would not miss too much. I never started anything new until 9:30, and I planned labs that could be finished in a shorter time.

My associate taught me the value of a good system of organization. He had all his notes and handouts for each unit of every course compiled in several binders, which then served as teaching guides. He supplemented the text with handouts, which frequently included newspaper and journal articles. I followed his lead; it provided an opportunity to tailor the students' printed information to what I was teaching, rather than having to tailor my teaching to fit the text.

One of the really valuable things I had a chance to explore was bringing technology into the classroom. The administration and staff were committed to using computers and technology as much as possible in the classroom. I was able to incorporate laser discs and even a computer game into my lessons, along with handouts taken from the Internet. I believe this strongly enhanced the students' learning.

One of the most interesting aspects of PT4 was the cooperation within the science department. Teachers with the same course shared their preparation periods; this meant they could keep all the classes in roughly the same place and make sure they were covering the same material. It also reduced the amount of preparation for everyone.

The most pleasant aspect of this placement for me was that I enjoyed the teaching immensely. Although I had three very different courses to deal with, I was not nervous. The teaching felt very comfortable, almost easy. My confidence in my teaching was at a point where I felt I could handle every situation that came up. It allowed me to be flexible; I could lead impromptu discussions in class, and I could set the pace and get the lesson back on track when it was required. It was fun.

Once more, multiculturalism was an issue. The school had a very large ESL population. In fact, many of the students already had university degrees, but were there to learn English. So once more I was reminded of the diversity of cultural backgrounds in the city and saw how that was reflected in the student population. As in my other placements, it was not reflected in the teacher population. By this time, I wasn't surprised at this disparity. Reflecting back on my experience, it concerns me that after only 8 weeks I would recognize this situation as the norm. It shows me how easy it is to become complacent about issues like this. I don't think anyone should accept that this is the norm and not be concerned about the message it sends to the students.

My final placement feels as though it was an affirmation of the knowledge and skills I've developed over this past year and of the teacher I am becoming. The teaching flowed very smoothly, even in classes with which I was unfamiliar. It was easy to get to know the students, and they seemed comfortable with me and with our relationship. In fact, I asked them to evaluate me and got a really positive response to my teaching style. I was very comfortable with my role in the classroom.

The issue of multiculturalism followed me through the year. I hope it continues to follow me. I've learned a lot about it this year, not only in terms of the reality among the students but also in terms of how other people view the issue and deal with it. Part of my role as a teacher is to keep this issue at the forefront, for the students and for my colleagues, and to learn how I can be a good teacher in classrooms where many different cultures are represented.

The next page in the album is blank, not because the journey has ended, but because the next part is unknown. But whatever comes next, it will continue to contribute to my growing sense of my professional self and my role as an educator. And whatever the next step is in this journey, it will not be the last step—this journey of professional development will continue throughout my teaching career.

Lessons to Live By

- Get involved. During practice teaching sessions, get involved in the school. Go to staff meetings and professional activity days. Attend relevant clubs. Meet the administration, and stay in touch with them and with your associate teachers when you leave. Get involved in extracurricular projects and in after-school activities with your associate teacher. Get to know as many of your colleagues, teachers, and professors as you can. They are valuable resources.
- Ask questions. Your associates like talking about teaching, and they will appreciate the fact that you want to learn more and that you value what they say. Also, ask for feedback early in your placement so that you can make any adjustments your associate suggests.
- Be confident. Students are very quick to sense when you are uncertain of what you're doing. Don't be afraid to tell them you

don't know the answer to something, but follow up on it by getting the answer for them (or challenging them to find the answer and enlighten you and the rest of the class).

- Know the content of the curriculum you are teaching. Find out in advance what you will be teaching, and make sure you understand it completely before you go into the classroom. Check the state, provincial, and board of education guidelines beforehand on the curriculum you will be teaching. Find out what texts the students are using and familiarize yourself with them. There's no substitute for really knowing and loving the subjects you teach.

 Reflecting, Responding, and Writing

1. Alicia describes her growth from a student of teaching concerned with "the mechanics of teaching—managing the workload, knowing students' names, running a class, shaping a lesson"—to a professional teacher who understands the relationship among content material, teaching strategies, and the multicultural context of schools. Describe your responses to her account of professional learning, and identify the parts that resonate for you. Describe your own journey from student to teacher—from someone who once thought like a student to someone who now thinks and acts like a teacher.
2. Alicia values opportunities to learn from experienced teachers, and she identifies many of the significant lessons she has learned in practical situations with experienced colleagues. She describes how she establishes collegial relationships with experienced teachers and asks for help, feedback, and professional advice. Identify the ways in which she does this.
3. Write about your own particular professional situation and what you have learned from experienced colleagues.
4. Describe the factors that enable you to learn from associate teachers and other experienced professionals in school settings.
5. Share your writing with a partner, discussing ways to establish good professional relations with experienced teachers and to learn from them. Describe those times when you have been successful in having others help you to learn things that you needed to know in school settings. Describe how you will use your existing knowledge to learn what you need to know.
6. With your partner, describe the obstacles you have had in establishing good collegial relationships with associate

teachers. Give each other feedback and suggestions for success in establishing and maintaining future professional relationships with experienced practitioners. Document your discussion.

7. Alicia valued the opportunity to bring technology into the classroom and to incorporate laser discs, computer games, and the Internet into her lessons to enhance students' learning. She knew that she was also supporting the school administration's and staff's commitment to technology in the classroom.

   - Describe any effort you have made to explore the use of technology in your classroom practices, and share your observations of the effects of this on students' learning.
   - Describe any effort you have made to incorporate the objectives and agendas of the school administration and staff into your classroom teaching.
   - Share your ideas with a partner, discussing the ways you have linked your individual purposes and interests with communal purposes and interests in a school. Describe the ways in which you have adapted what you do in the context of different schools and/or school systems.
   - Organize a class session on this topic, and share your ideas with colleagues. Discuss the benefits of being the kind of teacher who is a team player and good citizen in a school community.

8. Alicia's narrative is one of interactive learning, of sharing stories, ideas, and agendas. It is a story of resistance to isolation, solitary learning, entrenched views, and established ways of knowing and being. Her story challenges the "taken-for-granted" story of how things are in schools. Do you have a resistance story of your own? Do you have a story of collegial learning? Do you have stories of innovative and creative ways of working with colleagues, school administrators, parents, and others in school settings? Find examples of people like Alicia who are creating new narratives for their work in schools. Document these stories, and share them with your colleagues.

9. How does Alicia's story help you to think about your own story in new ways? How does it help you to think about teaching as a collegial, rather than an individualistic, endeavor? Reflect on these issues, and document your ideas and reflections.

10. How do the narratives by George, Gilbert, Ellen, and Alicia help you to think about how things might be otherwise in high school classrooms? How do they help you to think about a rescripted

role for the teacher in teacher-student relationships? How do they support your efforts to create relationships with students and professional colleagues and to work together toward common goals? How do these narratives inspire you to make positive changes in classrooms, schools, and school communities now and in your future career? Document your reflections as fully as possible, and explain how making new relations between existing ideas and structures, and making new kinds of relationships with students, colleagues, parents, community members, and others, can help you to achieve your goals.

11. Organize a large-group discussion on the topic "Creating Relationships and Making New Relations." Explore the topic by responding to the narratives in this section of the book and by identifying ways of incorporating the ideas, suggestions and strategies into classroom practices. Discuss your abilities to respond and to be responsible (response-able) in the context of relationships with students and professional colleagues. Discuss your abilities to "make new relations of the relations already at work in the environment in which [you] find [yourself]" (McDermott, 1986, p. 149). Document the main ideas of the discussion, and use them to provide direction for your professional growth.

Creating New Narratives: Connecting Self, School, and Society

Those who are teachers would have to accommodate ourselves to lives as clerks or functionaries if we did not have in mind a quest for a better state of things for those we teach and for the world we all share. It is simply not enough for us to reproduce the way things are.

MAXINE GREENE

The narratives in this section present portraits of beginning teachers who take seriously the idea of ethically based professional practice. They illustrate their authors' understanding of teaching as moral, ethical, and socially responsible work. These narratives present individuals who are willing to review the choices available to them, to question the status quo, to engage in critical and creative thinking, and to rescript the current and future stories of their professional lives. They show how the processes of inquiry have involved them in questioning their life histories, their socialization, and the ideologies and "official stories" being enacted around them. The inquiry process has enabled them to ask questions of their work, to find the patterns that give it meaning, and to replace individualistic and hierarchical scripts that isolate the teacher from students and colleagues, with scripts in which individual teachers cooperate with students, colleagues, parents, and community members.

These beginning teachers acknowledge that they are members of a school team whose combined expertise can achieve what cannot be done alone. They show how the difficulties and dilemmas of daily life in schools are handled through collaboration and shared problem solving. These

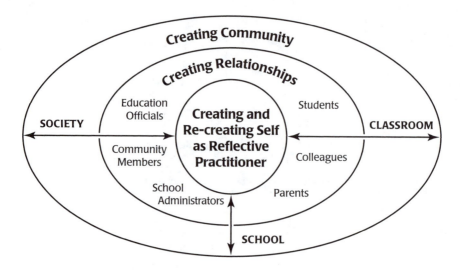

individuals are reformers rather than conformers: they have the willingness and capacities to reformulate the relationships, norms, and structures that restrict their freedom to teach in emancipatory and transformational ways. Their narratives provide invitations to readers to imagine how things might be otherwise in their own professional settings and to think about how shared values and ideals can be created through collaboration, negotiation, and shared decision making. The narratives are professional stories of hope, of possibility, and of seeking beyond the actual to a better order in classrooms, schools, and communities.

The prospective teachers here are attentive to the diversity of students in today's schools and sensitive to issues of equity, ethnicity, gender, and race in classroom and school settings. Their narratives illustrate some of the political, ethical, and moral dimensions of being a teacher, and the ways in which individual teachers bring their growing understanding of these issues to bear on decision making and on practical actions. They describe ways in which they worked to create inclusive, equitable, and just situations in their classrooms that benefit all students. They show how they collaborated with colleagues to make more significant connections between classrooms and schools and the larger societal, cultural, political, and global contexts around them. In addition, they recall how they enacted new scripts for the way individuals relate to each other in school settings—in teacher-student relationships, teacher-teacher relationships, teacher-administrator relationships, and school-community relationships.

Current scholarship in education has raised new awarenesses about the presence of many voices and viewpoints in schools and in society. It highlights the importance of diversity, inclusiveness, and the recognition of a multiplicity of perspectives. Current pedagogical theory emphasizes the importance of a curriculum design and of teaching strategies that replace hierarchical teacher-student relationships with relationships of mutual respect, shared authority, and the collaborative creation of knowledge. In this context, it becomes imperative for teachers to recognize each others' experiences and expertise and to collaborate with students, colleagues, parents, and other community members in the creation of learning environments where everyone's realities are recognized and valued. By respecting all voices—one's own and those of others—and by allowing multiple voices to be heard in the educational arena, prospective teachers learn to develop their own authentic voices and to be influenced but not overwhelmed by the voices of others. Through their efforts to create classroom and school communities where students learn to become full participants, these teachers continually develop their own abilities to rescript and enact new narratives of student-teacher relationships, of teacher-teacher relationships, and of classroom-school and community relations. Belenky, Clinchy, Goldberger, and Tarule (1986) describe this emancipatory kind of teaching, which emphasizes connection over separation, understanding and acceptance over judgment, and collaboration over debate. Teachers can teach in emancipatory ways if they "accord respect to and allow time for the knowledge that emerges from first hand experience; if instead of imposing their own expectations and arbitrary requirements, they encourage students to evolve their own patterns of work based on the problems they are pursuing" (p. 229).

In chapter 10, Jana Weerasinghe addresses the development of the political and ethical dimensions of a prospective teacher's professional knowledge. Jana's narrative addresses these issues:

- The purpose of schools in a democratic society and the role of the teacher in this context
- The question of whose knowledge is worthwhile in the school curriculum (Who benefits from this, and who faces disadvantages?)
- The balance of freedom and control in teaching and learning
- Equitable classrooms: working toward shared decision making, shared leadership, and the creation of shared values in teaching
- Inclusiveness, equity, social justice, and minority voices in the democratic classroom

In chapter 11, John Morrissey presents a narrative account dealing with a "critical incident" in this beginning teacher's life. The incident had a significant impact on John's professional learning and on his understanding of what it means to be a teacher. His account addresses the following issues:

- The ethical, moral, cultural, social, and political dimensions of teaching
- Ways to deal with conflict through relationships

- Respect, care, and compassion in teacher-student and teacher-teacher relationships
- The teacher as artist: searching for truth and authenticity through self-directed inquiry
- The creation of collegial, collaborative learning communities

In chapter 12, Ruth Weinstock focuses on the role of the teacher as community builder. Ruth's narrative addresses these issues:

- The creation of new scripts for the teacher, classroom structures and cultures, the school, and the school community
- The balance and reconciliation of tradition and innovation, of conforming and reforming
- The co-creation of shared values and purposes in community
- Interdependent, intergenerational, and interorganizational relations the teacher as leader in the creation and maintenance of a moral universe.

CHAPTER 10

Teaching Transformations: Merging Self and Teacher

Everybody wants to be right in a world where there ain't no right or wrong to be found. My side. He don't listen to my side. She don't listen to my side. Just like that chicken coop, everything has got four sides; his side, her side, an outside and an inside. All of it is the truth. But that takes a lot of work. . . . When getting at the truth starts to hurt, it's easier to turn away.

GLORIA NAYLOR

Jana Weerasinghe's narrative is about one beginning teacher's growing awareness of the ways in which politics and ethics are embedded in the daily practices of classrooms. She explores the political, cultural, and ethical dimensions of her own professional knowledge and practices. As an immigrant to Canada from Sri Lanka and a member of a "patriarchal home," Jana speaks of her growing awareness of multicultural and socioeconomic issues as they pertain to education. She acknowledges the importance of voice, control, and self-confidence in the context of teaching, learning, and learning to teach.

Jana describes the way in which she reconceptualized her understanding of the teacher's role and transformed her thinking regarding the purpose of schools in a multicultural and democratic society. Her narrative describes her efforts to change her practices in the light of this understanding, to focus on creating a better balance between structure and control in her teaching, and to create an equitable and democratic learning environment for all the students in her classroom.

Jana's narrative speaks to the necessity for new learning and for "unlearning" as part of the process of professional growth. Her account illustrates the dynamic interplay between theory and practice as she

129

reconsiders her opinions and ideas in the context of her interactions with students and colleagues, and of her ongoing inquiry. She describes her difficulties in creating a democratic classroom given that her prior educational experiences had been in traditional, hierarchical classrooms. Her narrative addresses the way she accepted the need to question what she thought, to reconstruct her understandings, and to become more confident about trying out new teaching strategies. It illustrates the ways in which she worked to adapt her teaching methods so that her students could develop their voices and practice the skills, strategies, and ways of thinking that would enable them to participate actively in a democratic society. Jana questions the practice of grouping students according to their intellectual abilities and comes to agree with a controversial policy requiring students of all levels to take classes together during the first year of high school. Her self-directed inquiry results in changes and in what she describes as the transformation of herself as a teacher.

How Did I Come to Develop Such a Strong, Protective Outer Shell?

by Jana Weerasinghe

Looking back on my early experiences as a teacher, I have asked myself this question. Since that time, I have learned as much about the person I am as I have about the students I teach through the ongoing process of self-evaluation. Throughout my life, I have always had a strong need to control every facet of my existence. I guess it was a form of self-preservation. I have always feared being controlled by those around me. I believe this fear is an offshoot of having grown up in a very patriarchal home, where for so long my voice was cast aside. The tightly woven, seemingly impregnable outer coating allowed me to develop inside it, while scarcely allowing others to harm me. I believe this desire for control had a profound effect on how I saw the world around me and the people in it.

The path to this point in my life has not been without a measure of pain. Reflecting on my personal strengths and shortcomings has been a tiresome yet uplifting journey. It has been necessary for me to find out who I am as a person to know who I am as a teacher.

Putting Theory into Practice

I began to think about my own beliefs and to see how seriously flawed they are. . . . Before my teacher education program, I was a major supporter of the idea that the school's main role should be to supply workers for the economy. Therefore, I assumed that the advanced, basic, and general levels in high school all accurately corresponded to an area in the labor market. Furthermore, I believed that merit alone dictated which level a student would be placed in. Thus, I felt that the more able, advanced-level students would go on to college and hold the elite jobs in society, while the general and basic students would make their way to the manual jobs in society. I had never stopped to consider the idea that students were streamed into these different levels in schools because of numerous reasons, having nothing to do with ability, but that I now understand as having to do with racial and socioeconomic biases. These influences separate students into groups in the future society in which they will live. It was only after reading about the practice of streaming students according to their intellectual abilities and the reasons for it that I began to think about my own beliefs regarding this practice and to see how seriously flawed they are. The most striking argument against my view was put forth by one of my colleagues during a class when she pointed out that she had a learning disability and that this should not hold her or others like her from reaching their potential. I was seriously moved by her honesty and forthrightness. She got me thinking.

During my first practice teaching session, I had the opportunity to work in three multilevel classes. What I found was that many of the so-called general-level students were capable of producing good work (as many of their test scores and class presentations indicated). However, many of these students seemed to believe that they could never be advanced students, and they lacked self-esteem and a sense of self-worth. One student in particular was convinced that he was "dumb," yet his presentation was one of the best I had the opportunity to see. It was this young man more than anyone else who forced me to question the practice of separating high school students into basic level, general level, and advanced level classes during their high school years. Mike only thought he could not succeed because society labels general- and basic-level students as less capable of success. But I thought about how the word *success* is so value laden and socially constructed. What constitutes success? Who decides who is successful and why? Perhaps if people like myself could get out of the habit of determining a person's worth by the mark he or she gets on a test, we could improve the students' self-esteem.

I have changed the way I look at the role of schools in society. The initiative to destream grade 9 classes in Ontario has been a highly controversial issue. I now see it as a way to give students an additional year before they are segregated into streams. It allows them to get accustomed to the high school structures and routines before they are placed in the different levels of classes for subsequent years. The idea of the school as a producer of laborers is an outdated and aggressive notion. One of the main goals of education should be to strive for equality and for individuals' rights to be the best they can be. However, I've realized that early streaming prevents students from reaching this goal.

Changing Your Script to Meet the Needs of Students

"What was wrong with them?" I asked myself.

During my practice teaching sessions, I learned a lot about students. Prior to teaching full-time, I felt that if a student didn't want to do the work I assigned, it was because he or she was lazy. If a student received a low test score, it was because he or she failed to understand the material. I never questioned my method of teaching as having an effect on how and what students learn. I believed that the Socratic style of teaching was a very effective way to get a point across, especially since it is the way I myself learn best.

During one of my practice teaching sessions, I was in charge of teaching "Frontier Experiences of Settlement" to a group of Ontario Academic Credits (OAC) history students. I decided that because this course was a preparation course for university, I would conduct a 75-minute lecture on the topic. After the class left the room, my associate came up to me and calmly asked, "How many [students] do you think actually got anything out of that? Did you notice that Johnny fell asleep in class?" I was upset. I truly believed that the lecture was an effective way to teach students. I was annoyed by the lack of interest the students showed in material I found fascinating. "What was wrong with them?" I asked myself.

That night I went home and decided I would try a new strategy in the classroom. I would try two-way communication or a question-answer lesson. The next day I asked the students questions based on the readings I had them do for homework. Furthermore, I asked individual students to take over my role by explaining key concepts to the class. I used the roll-down map to have students visually demonstrate the settlement pattern of the early settlers. I allowed the students to see that history could be fun if they would only allow themselves to open up to it. I remember dancing around the room and inviting students to take part in the class. One student named Ilan came up to me after class and said, "Miss Weerasinghe, your energy is contagious." It was a small beginning, but I learned a lot from this experience. I learned that students need to be made a part of the lesson. They need to be invited to share their answers with each other. More importantly, I learned that if I make my class more interesting for them, they may develop an interest in learning history. They may learn without even knowing they are doing so, and they may find it so interesting that they can't help but become involved. I also learned about cooperative learning and I decided to give it a try. What did I have to lose?

I remember being a student in the school system and seeing group work as the time when I did the work for the entire group. I was biased about this method, and my opinion prevented me from trying it in my own classroom for quite a time. However, I decided to try it with a group of grade 12 economics students. I found that when properly structured and monitored by the teacher, cooperative learning is a way of interesting students in the material and allowing them an opportunity to investigate issues or problems for themselves. I also used an inquiry process into current events to entice students to look at the changes in the Soviet economy. Moving away from the standard textbook examples to the real world seemed to tweak the students' interests.

Instead of setting myself up as the authority on the topic, I began to let the students investigate the subject with input from me only when needed. The results were amazing. Students who would not talk in class were now actively volunteering information and personal comments on the questions I asked them to focus on. ESL (English as a Second Language) students who had failed the test and who had been very quiet in class were now participating in group discussions. These experiences were my teachers, and they proved to me what I had heard in my university classes: there are different learning styles, and I need to be aware of this fact and incorporate them into my lesson plans. Mr. M, one of my associates, showed me that we need to challenge kids to form opinions on issues of importance to them and to society, and to give them plenty of opportunities to express their opinions and ideas.

Instead of Giving Them the Answer, Give Them the Question

Mr. M suggested that I should allow kids to inquire. Theory and practice came together for me when I saw for myself that cooperative learning allows students to learn for themselves. The inquiry process gives students ownership and responsibility for their education. The implication of these insights for me was that I had to rethink my role as a teacher. I had to figure out ways to allow students to question the world around them and to become well-informed citizens. I also had to admit to myself that for far too long, I had projected the standards that I expected from myself onto the students I teach.

Transforming Myself as a Teacher

> *When I came into the program I was a cocky, overconfident, and overly arrogant person, yet I would have described myself at that time as "open-minded." Now I see that this word truly could not be used to describe me as I was then.*

The incident that caused me to reevaluate my perception of students was when I had a student named Joy in my class. Joy came to me the day an essay was due. She explained to me that no matter how hard she tried, she still did not understand the material. In her words, she "couldn't do it." She showed me her outline for the paper. I realized it was not that she didn't understand the material but that she lacked the self-confidence to admit to herself she could write the paper. We talked at length after school. I asked probing questions that she answered quite easily. I showed her she had all the pieces to the puzzle, but she lacked the picture to put it together. I helped her to organize her points and gently cajoled her into developing her thesis and providing the supporting evidence. Throughout the whole session, I kept telling her she was as smart as anyone else in the class and she "could do it!"

The next day she gave me her paper. After marking it, I gave her an A and wrote in big print across the front page, "Congratulations, Joy, I told you, you could do it!!!!!" After class she came up to me beaming with delight. She said, "Thank you," and I quickly said, "For what? You did all the work." I smiled back at her. With that, not another word was said about the matter, for I wanted Joy to realize that success in school wasn't a mystery or something reserved for the chosen few. Anyone can do well if they learn to trust themselves.

Finally, when I look at the changes I have made to my perceptions and my understanding, I would have to say I have changed my image of myself and my image of me the teacher. When I came into the program, I was a cocky, overconfident, and overly arrogant person, yet I would have described myself at that time as "open-minded." Now I see that this word truly could not be used to describe me as I was then. I rarely took other people's ideas seriously, and I saw my own viewpoints as having huge value and importance. Now, as I reflect on this time, I think my need for control had a lot to do with my need to have students take my point of view as the gospel.

My experiences taught me I was wrong to think kids would readily accept my opinion as law. When students disagreed with me, I was no longer deeply offended. Even with my 4 years of university, I have come to see that I can learn a lot from the students I teach. It has taken me a long time to open up to the ideas of others. Others' ideas don't seem as threatening as they once did. Just as a student must learn to look at a subject from many different angles, I am learning to listen and understand the ideas and points of view of others as well. I have also discovered it is OK to show the students how much I love to learn by asking questions myself and by letting students know I don't know everything and I don't have all the answers. It is this need to know and to find out that makes me enjoy learning. Perhaps through my own excitement I can inspire others to investigate history, or society, or whatever other topic or questions face them.

I'm still wondering about how to give students control over their learning without having them pulling off my wings. To investigate this question, I experimented with giving them varying degrees of control over their own learning. For example, during one of my practice teaching sessions, I allowed the students to take most of the control over their investigation of various topics with little input from me. I let the kids talk in class, go to the washroom whenever they wanted, or head to the library during class time. When I asked students to give me feedback on my teaching at the end of the session, I was very surprised to hear that I had given them too much control. They said they had needed more guidance! I realized that students themselves want to be given limits to what they can and can't do in class. I also have realized that I need to reflect constantly on the needs of each individual class and to recognize that some classes may need more control than others.

Restructuring the Self around the Community

To the Buddha, "everything in the universe is impermanent." Thus life, matter, states of being, and states of knowledge or understanding are forever changing. The year I spent at a faculty of education was one in which I went through a gradual transformation in the way I view myself as a person and as a teacher. When I reflect on the past year, I feel as though I have awakened from a long, restless sleep. Through my experiences in teaching, my talks with teachers, my classes, and my reading, I have been transformed from my cocoonlike existence into a butterfly who is open-minded, free to explore the world, and not firmly planted to any one place or way of doing things.

It was a year in which I learned to open myself to the ideas of others and to see things from a multitude of different angles. I let go of my old views of the role of the school as supplying workers for the economy. Also I changed my views of students who do not hold my beliefs or who refuse to work, as lazy or dumb. Furthermore, I learned that there are numerous different ways of learning. More surprising to me, however, are the changes I have seen in my image of myself and my understanding of my role as a teacher.

One bright and sunny September day in 1992, I walked into a foundations class at a faculty of education. At the time I remember looking around the room and thinking, "I deserve to be here . . . and I think I can fix everything that ails the education system. Just ask me!" I was arrogant, conceited, and more than a bit self-righteous. I believed I had all the qualities to make me the ideal teacher for young people today. I was young, intelligent, "open-minded," and I came from a good home. I felt I had all the answers, and people in the faculty and in the schools could learn from me. However, I have altered this self-indulgent portrait of myself through my experiences and the new understanding I gained.

I still have a lot of trouble giving up control of the classroom to the students, and it suits me much better to have what I call "structured control" as a means of dealing with my inability to fully release my grip on the reins. I look for ways to provide a balance between structure and freedom. For example, I give students projects to investigate, but I also give them focus questions around which I want them to inquire. The students are learning independently while I still maintain some control over what goes on in the classroom.

These changes have had an effect on my whole person. I have had to do some unlearning as well as learning and it has made me more confident in my ability to learn. I am happy with who I am, and I am not as concerned as I had been about how other people see me. I am more willing to stand up for myself, even in my personal life (although I have more progress to make in this area). Most valuable of all is my realization that I no longer need to be "perfect" in everything I do. No longer do I need to evaluate myself according to my rigid preset list of attributes that made up what I pictured as the ideal teacher and woman.

I am still as passionate about teaching as I was back in September. Along the way I have learned a great deal about my image of schools, students, and, more important, myself, Jana, the person and the teacher. I am ready to fly, and I have shed the cocoon that protected me for so many years. My wings feel strong enough to make the long journey that lies before me. One thing is certain: I will continue to learn much along the way.

Reflecting, Responding, and Writing

1. Describe Jana's narrative in your own words: "It is the story of a prospective teacher who . . . " Continue this phrase.
2. Jana explains that she went through a gradual transformation during the teacher education program, during which she let go of some of her old views of the role of the teacher, the students, and the school. By listening to others' perspectives, she transformed her understandings. She learned to create a new narrative for herself as teacher, for the role of the student, and for the school.
   - Describe the changes you have witnessed in your thinking about schools, students, and yourself as teacher. Write about these changes and the events or experiences that stimulated the changes. Identify the major sources of your significant learning experiences—practical experiences, readings, conversations, arguments, discussions, workshops.
   - Share these stories of learning with a group of your colleagues. Reflect on the similarities and differences among the stories, and on the meanings as they pertain to your own ongoing inquiry. Document the main ideas that emerge from the discussion.
3. Jana's learning involves "unlearning." The unlearning of one belief, such as her view that "the school's main role is to supply workers for the economy," has implications for her understanding of the role of the student, the role of the teacher, and the role of classroom setting as a place of learning. Describe an incident of "unlearning" in your own professional education and the follow-up questions and inquiry.
   - Write about the new questions raised because of what you unlearned.
   - Share your writing with a trusted colleague.

- Analyze your writing for insights into the future learning
  you wish to do. Reflect on your analysis and document your
  reflections.
4. Jana deals with the issues of control, freedom, and responsibility.
   She describes how she learned to be responsive to students'
   voices and to focus her teaching on helping students to engage
   in inquiry. She describes her struggle to create a learning
   environment where there is a balance between structure and
   freedom. Describe the ways in which you create classroom
   situations and settings that give students opportunities for
   developing their voices and for self-directed inquiry. How
   do your students practice decision making, form their own
   opinions, negotiate with others, choose from among possible
   options, and take responsibility for their choices, initiate
   questions for inquiry, resolve conflicts, and create schemes and
   strategies for collaborative work? What obstacles do you
   encounter in encouraging this self-direction in students'
   learning? What successes have you had? Discuss these issues
   with your colleagues and document the discussions.
5. Write about your understanding of the role of public schools in
   a democratic society.
   - Describe the purposes of schools, providing a rationale for
     your ideas.
   - How does your conception of what schools should be
     coincide with the reality of your experiences in schools?
   - What are the assumptions and "taken-for-granteds" being
     enacted in the schools you have experienced?
   - What changes do you plan to make in your classroom, in
     your school, and in your school community that will enable
     students to practice the habits that are central to democratic
     learning and living?
   - Describe the ways you will help students to make connections
     between their own interests and those of the school and social
     communities in which they live.
   - Document your ideas, wonderings, questions, and plans for
     future action.

CHAPTER 11

Confronting Challenge
with Creativity, Collegiality,
and Compassion

The challenge is to make the ground palpable and visible to our students, to make possible the interplay of multiple voices, of "not quite commensurable visions." It is to attend to the plurality of consciousness—and their recalcitrances and their resistances, along with their affirmations, their "songs of love." And, yes, it is to work for responsiveness to principles of equity, principles of equality, and principles of freedom, which still can be named within the contexts of caring and concern. The principles and the contexts have to be chosen by living human beings against their own life-worlds, and in the light of their lives with others, by persons able to call, to say, to sing, and—using their imaginations, tapping their courage—to transform.

MAXINE GREEN

John Morrissey's narrative deals with one prospective teacher's response to issues of racism, homophobia, and censorship in the context of his practice teaching. The narrative highlights the political, moral, and ethical context in which the daily acts of teaching take place, in which teachers respond to students and others, deal with practical dilemmas, and make decisions. John's narrative raises issues about the responsibilities of teachers and of school administrators to deal with racial discrimination, homophobia, and incidents of abuse, in a collaborative and collegial way. He recalls how he collaborated with his experienced colleagues in the school to turn a potentially negative situation into a learning experience for all those involved.

John's narrative offers a portrait of the prospective teacher as a teacher-leader who deals with dilemmas and difficulties collaboratively and creatively, and whose practices are grounded in an ethic of compassion and care. It highlights the importance of ongoing inquiry in a teacher's life and the necessity for teachers to examine their thinking and practices continually for indications of insensitivity, bias, fearfulness, and complacency. John emphasizes the importance of a supportive network of colleagues in every teacher's life and of dealing with challenges through creativity, compassion, and collegiality.

Reflections on a Critical Incident in Practice

by John Morrissey

The incidents and their resolution also gave me the opportunity to see how socially and politically sensitive issues were handled in that school and to reflect on my role in the process.

The ethical, moral, cultural, social, and political dimensions of teaching are with us constantly, so it's easy to find classroom examples of how teachers must face them. As in journalism, law, medicine, or any other profession that involves working with the public and making decisions that involve others (it's hard to think of a profession that doesn't, really), these dimensions make up a great part of teaching. When I started writing this essay during one of my practice sessions, I hadn't chosen a single major incident on which to reflect and had planned to write about a series of smaller events. Then two related classroom incidents raised issues of race, sexual orientation, and harassment and caused me to change my plans. The incidents and their resolution also gave me the opportunity to see how socially and politically sensitive issues were handled in that school and to reflect on my role in the process.

To begin, *incidents* may be too strong a word for the classroom exchanges that raised these issues for me. What struck me was the fact that I heard remarkably similar comments and concerns raised in two different grade 9 classes by two groups of students. The remarks were made independently and spontaneously by the two groups of students, with no coaxing from me. I was struck by how all five of these pupils—three in one class, two in another—seemed to be singing from the same hymnbook. The five knew one another and may well have been talking together outside class. All five students happened to be black, and at least three were from West Indian families.

I passed my classroom observations on to my associate teacher and his response, coupled with that of the school administration, gave me plenty of food for thought. Let me underline here that I was struck by the positive and thoughtful nature of my associate's responses during and after the incidents

I will describe. My associate wasn't present for the first exchange, but he was in the classroom for the second.

I wanted to squelch what I saw as an ugly bit of bigotry intruding into the classroom.

To set the scene, my practicum was at a public high school known for its rich ethnic, racial, and linguistic variety. The teachers and administration promote and take advantage of that richness. In the classes in which I took part, discussion was always tailored to take note of the international and multicultural angles in the curriculum. For example, the classes I worked with included students of Balkan, Latin American, Caribbean, East Indian, Middle Eastern, Pakistani, Chinese, and Vietnamese background, some of whom had been in Canada for as little as 2 years.

At this school, two grade 9 classes with which I was involved were undergoing a mandatory, provincial test of their reading and writing ability. The test, which was scheduled to take up 10 full periods, was a lengthy and laborious process dreaded by students and teachers alike. In maintaining a positive atmosphere and keeping the class focused, my associate and I had challenges equal to those faced by the students. Ironically, this theme of challenges was woven throughout the writing exercises in the test.

In one grade 9 class were two youths I'll call Greg and Jamie. Greg was a bright young man who'd apparently decided against wasting his valuable time on the provincial test. Jamie pretty much followed Greg's lead, and the two of them had enough influence with their peers—and loud enough voices—to disrupt the entire class. After helping to administer the test for 2 weeks, I can't say I entirely blame Greg for holding the exercise in contempt. It was clear to me that my associate would have preferred to have devoted those 10 classes to course work. As happens in so many jobs, we were stuck carrying out a task we neither wanted nor approved of. My associate was professional enough to do the work without telegraphing his personal opinions to the students, and I followed suit. Whether it's possible—or even desirable—to conceal one's opinion from one's students is another question.

Anyway, Greg and Jamie would try just about any gambit to get the focus of the class away from the test—including teasing or tormenting the girls who sat in front of them or asking me particularly pointed or off-topic questions. For example, the test often asked what challenges students faced and how they had dealt with them. Greg sent the class into hysterics one day by asking me whether having a gay teacher would be considered a challenge. While Greg was saying this, another student shouted out, to more laughter, that the girls' gym teacher, whom she named, was a lesbian.

I had been walking around the classroom talking with students at their desks, so I stepped up to Greg and made eye contact with him.

"This gay teacher you're asking me about—assuming he was gay, which you have no way of knowing—was he a good teacher?"

"Yes, he was," Greg answered with a knowing smirk, "but he was still gay."

"That doesn't matter," I replied. "In this school we don't judge people by their sexual orientation, or their race, or their culture, or their language. Hating or excluding somebody because you think they're gay is the same thing as discriminating against somebody because they're black or white or Asian or whatever. What really matters is what people do and how we treat each other. What do you say to that?"

"That's good. Hey, sir, did you ever have any gay teachers when you were in school?"

"If I did, I wouldn't have known, and it wouldn't have mattered anyway."

"You know where Green Street is, sir? You ever been there?"

"Sure, I've been there, Greg, lots of times. I know what you're getting at—it's the gay district. So what? It's also a major downtown street. Now it's time to get back to work. We've only got about 15 minutes left to do this section of the test, and I can see from your paper you still have plenty of work to do."

I knew from the start of our exchange that Greg was trying to bait me by implying that I was a gay teacher, but I was determined not to play his game. I didn't like Greg's attitude. I wanted to squelch what I saw as an ugly bit of bigotry intruding into the classroom. At the same time, I wanted to do this quickly because the class was falling behind in their test work and an extended argument was just the kind of disruption Greg wanted to create.

Later in the same class I overheard a bit of an interesting argument between Greg and a girl I'll call Noelle. Noelle was criticizing him for something he'd done or for the company he kept, saying there were some Jamaicans "with their crime and their hip-hop culture" who incited a backlash against other Jamaicans and black people in general. Greg argued that she was being unfair to him and his friends, that people new to this country deserve a break because they faced more prejudice and were being unfairly blamed for crime.

I told them this sounded like a good topic for a debate or for pieces of writing in their writing folders, since they were bringing up significant and topical issues about racism, immigration, and crime. They both snorted at that, but they seemed pleasantly surprised to hear that other people might be interested in what they thought. I doubted Greg would actually write about this, but I saw a gleam in Noelle's eye as she turned back to her test work.

> *He believed students should have the right to "use their fists" to protect themselves from "gay teachers."*

I was very surprised the next day when a trio of students in the second grade 9 class raised the "gay teacher challenge" again. A very bright but taciturn student I'll call Stan (who, like Greg, was less than thrilled with the test but, unlike Greg, tended to apply himself a bit better) put "gay teachers" at the top of his list—along with "racist teachers" and "abusive teachers." I was fascinated to hear my associate asking Stan about this view.

"This is very serious stuff, Stan," he said. "I certainly hope there aren't any teachers in this school who treat anyone in a racist or abusive way. If there are, I'd like to know about it."

At this moment, another student I'll call Corinna loudly repeated the allegation that the girls' gym teacher was a lesbian, also naming the teacher. "She takes attendance in the shower, eee-yew," Corinna grimaced. Another student, whom I'll call Tina, chimed in to support Corinna. There was a teacher who kept touching her lightly on the shoulder even though she'd told the teacher she didn't like this, Tina said. Stan added he believed students should have the right to "use their fists" to protect themselves from "gay teachers."

After some discussion, my associate brought the class back to order and got them working on the test again.

Later, I was amused to hear Stan say to Tina when she asked him a spelling question: "No, it's *racist.* R-A-C-I-S-T. Don't you know how to spell that yet?"

After the class, I told my associate I had been struck by the similarity between the outbursts in the two classes—the concern about gay teachers and especially the repeated naming of one particular teacher. I filled him in on what had happened in the first class and my reaction to it. I was concerned on two counts: First, if the students' remarks were genuine, they could indicate a serious problem in teacher behavior that would, by law, have to be dealt with. Second, if the students' remarks were frivolous—that is, if they were based on misunderstandings or rumor-mongering or were just intended to provoke a couple of white, middle-class teachers—we had a student behavior problem that could eventually threaten a teacher's job.

> *If there is racism or sex abuse in the school, we as teachers are bound by law to deal with it.*

The next day, my associate told me he'd been thinking about the exchanges and had even spoken to the school principal about them. He and the principal agreed, he told me, that it was important to talk to the five students outside class. In addition, my associate said, the principal had asked to see copies of the test writing by the students that had raised these concerns. This news gave me a chill, especially since, as a writer, teacher, and former journalist, I am opposed to censorship or what's called "prior restraint"—that is, giving an authority figure the power to veto what someone else writes. However, my associate pointed out that although the principal had asked to see the tests, he had not yet handed them over and still hoped to avoid doing so by resolving the situation with the students first. To my associate's credit, that's just what happened.

My associate told me he intended to call the five students out of their classes that afternoon to meet them as a group in the office. The idea was to discuss the significance of the issues raised in their test work and the discussions in class and to remind them that there was a formal process they could turn to if they felt they had been discriminated against or had been sexually or physically abused.

When the five came into the office, I could see they were tense and not about to give anything away. The very experience of coming into the teachers' office was a bit intimidating for them. Stan, Jamie, and Greg slouched in their seats. Stan pulled the hood of his fleece jacket over his head, and all five students initially avoided making eye contact with me or my associate. However, as my associate spoke, I could feel the students relax and see their gaze coming up from their feet. He reminded them that this meeting was not a punishment but an attempt to communicate about important issues the students had raised in class. He focused on three areas: how we get along together in the school as a community, the legal obligation of teachers to report and act on any evidence of racial discrimination or of abuse, and the process students can follow if they have a genuine complaint to make. He told them of his pride in the record of racial harmony at the school. He said he was confident in the ability of students and teachers to work out any racial tensions through classroom discussion and mutual learning.

When he invited the students' comments, Corinna said, "Say some more, sir." She and Tina were looking up, and even Greg was making eye contact with me and my associate. If there is racism, abuse, or sex abuse in the school, we as teachers are bound by law to deal with it, he told them. If these are just stories, we don't want them to get out of hand and maybe even cost a teacher's job, but we do want to deal with real problems.

Corinna asked some questions about the sexual harassment complaint process. My associate was very familiar with the process, and he told the students he felt secure in its justice and confidentiality. He also noted that making an allegation of abuse was a serious matter and not something to be done lightly.

I was given a chance to speak and told the students I had been struck by the similarity of the comments in the two classes. I noted that since I was in their classroom for only 2 weeks, I knew I couldn't be a big part of their lives. Nonetheless, I told them, I was struck by the number of interesting things they had to say about how issues such as racism affected their lives, and I hoped they would share their insights with the rest of us by writing about them. I also wanted to make the point that gay bashing is a kind of bigotry, and all forms of bigotry are equally odious.

After the students had returned to class—with a more relaxed air than they had shown on the way to the office—my associate said he "felt good about them." He agreed with my concern that they could have felt overwhelmed by the situation, but he "felt the hard shell crumbling," as their defensiveness melted away.

Upon reflection I resolved that no matter what our skin colors, they were still my students and I was still their teacher.

The next step in the process, if the students had produced any firm allegations, would have been to have them talk to the principal. That step wasn't needed, my associate said, and neither did the principal need to see the students' writings. However, he did have a follow-up of his own. The situation had shown him, he said, that the grade 9 students were not fully aware of three important things: the school and the school board's commitment to an antiracist curriculum, the school's sexual harassment or abuse complaint process, and the legal responsibilities of teachers. In response, my associate decided to draw up a teaching unit on these very topics for his grade 9 classes. What's more, he announced in class the next day his plan to introduce the unit and his rationale for it—that the students need to know where the school and the teachers stand, both by law and by inclination, on racism and human rights issues.

Finding My Way as a Teacher, My Voice as a Writer, and My Vision as an Artist

In analyzing this incident, I've been struck by the way my associate's actions, in terms of both the students and the school system, reflected qualities I want to develop in my own teaching. With the students, his tone throughout (and mine as well, I hope) was measured, respectful, caring, and just. He listened attentively to what the students were saying but didn't back down from telling them when they'd crossed the line of what was fair or acceptable. With the system, he kept in touch with his principal as the situation developed, receiving both advice and support. Backup from the office might have been helpful if anyone had been so intimidated by the process of meeting that they had accused us of browbeating the students or even of subjecting them to undue attention because of race.

This last factor was on my mind because I wondered whether my perception of the students and their comments was influenced by any hint of racism on my part. Was I playing the white boss man in this case? Upon reflection I resolved that no matter what our skin colors, they were still my students and I was still their teacher, and as such I had a responsibility to them to be alert for real complaints and to take a strong stand against bigotry of any kind.

I was glad my associate had managed not to give the principal copies of the students' writing. Handing the writings over was something I believe I couldn't have done because it might compromise my students' confidentiality, even though they were writing for a provincial test. I believe that if I truly want the students to keep on writing, they must know (and so must I) that they can trust me with what they write. My associate, who evidently held the same belief, managed to honor his principles without alienating his principal.

Also, I was very impressed with the fact that my associate turned a ticklish situation into a learning opportunity for me and for the two grade 9 classes. He included me in the process of dealing with the situation that I had pointed out to him. The situation became an opportunity for me to learn more about what kind of teacher I want to be and how I can work with real students in the existing system. It also contributed to my own lifelong antiracist education process. If I want to battle bigotry and injustice in others, I must always be on the lookout for them in myself and in my teaching.

Prejudice and denial . . . are the enemies of creativity on the personal and the collective levels.

In polite, adult, white, middle-class company (which is where I find myself most of the time), people tend to avoid such topics as racism and homophobia—perhaps because we don't want to lose friendships over "pointless" arguments or because we don't want to question ourselves too closely on these matters. This polite silence, also known as denial, makes it harder for members of the dominant culture to recognize and deal with their own prejudices, let alone those of others.

Yet, as a teacher, those of us who are polite, straight, white middle-class people will find our students—many of whom come from groups with which we are unfamiliar or against whom we may harbor active or latent prejudices—are all too willing to bring up taboo subjects. Even more troubling, the students are as likely to express prejudice themselves as they are to bemoan it.

I want my classes to be safe, welcoming, just, enjoyable, creative, and liberating places for both me and my students. Prejudice and denial—the cleaving to received ideas and the rejection of new ones or the fear of taking risks that might expose our own weaknesses—are the enemies of creativity on the personal and the collective levels.

To find my way as a teacher, my voice as a writer, or my vision as an artist (for these are three aspects of one thing), I must overcome the ingrained denial, the self-censorship, that keeps me from seeing myself and the world around me as clearly as I can. This is not to make my point of view somehow more objective or enlightened than that of anyone else—both, happily, are impossibilities—but to make it more truly my own and, in doing so, to make myself more fully human.

This experience leads me toward a model for the process of becoming the type of teacher I feel I can best be. That model is of the teacher as a kind of artist. I don't mean this in the pejorative sense of "artistic" as a precious or vague or capital-S sensitive, although authentic sensitivity is an important tool for the job. What I mean to become is a teacher (and writer and artist) whose own unleashed creative thought and energy, directed through the craft and discipline of teaching, can help to stimulate the creative thought and energy of others.

Reflecting, Responding, and Writing

1. How do you respond to John's narrative personally and professionally? Identify the most important things you learned from this account of professional learning. What have you learned about the value of having a supportive network of colleagues in your professional life?

2. John's narrative illustrates one teacher's attempts to reframe the story of how things take place in classrooms and schools. Describe how he has rescripted the role of the teacher. Describe the ways in which this changed role for the teacher affects teacher-student relationships, teacher-teacher relationships, and teacher-school administrator relationships. Share your ideas with a colleague, and document your discussion.

3. With a colleague, identify a moral, political, or ethical dilemma you have encountered in your professional life. Explain how you dealt with it and the results of your actions. What did you learn from the experience? Describe the incident, the way you dealt with it, and what you learned from the experience. Document the main ideas of the discussion in writing.

4. John was sympathetic to students' disinterest in the mandatory test being administered, yet he understood that his professional role required him not to telegraph his personal opinions to the students. He wonders whether it is possible or even desirable to conceal one's opinions from students.
   • What do you think of this issue? Explain and provide a rationale for your stance.
   • Pair up with a colleague who takes a different stance on the issue, and outline each perspective in detail.
   • Write about your ideas on the issue after the discussion, and explain how you will deal with a specific issue such as this (having to do something in your classroom that you do not personally agree with or that students do not value or want to do) in your future professional practice.
   • Analyze what you have written from legal, ethical, moral, and professional perspectives.

5. John describes the affective dimensions of confronting the challenge he faced. He acknowledges his need to be compassionate and just, and to be ethical and confidential in his interactions with students. Describe a parallel situation

from your own experience, and explain how you maintained (and possibly nurtured) relations with students in the process of dealing with a conflict, or in resolving a sensitive issue.

6. John describes his focus as a teacher, a writer, and an artist. He explains that these aspects of himself are united in focusing his creative thought and energy on his teaching and on stimulating the creative thought and energy of others.
   - How do you respond to this philosophy of teaching?
   - Do you have a unifying focus for your teaching?
   - Describe the benefits and difficulties associated with linking your vision of the teacher you want to be to the realities of the practical situations you have experienced.
   - Share your reflections with a partner, and document the major ideas that are discussed.

7. Retell this incident from the beginning from the perspective of one of the students.
   - Explain your part in the incident, what you said and did, and how you felt throughout.
   - Explain how you feel after the event and your attitude and feelings toward both of the teachers in the incident.
   - Give advice to the teachers about dealing with conflict in classrooms and schools.

8. The teachers in this story used the incident as a "teachable moment" and made it the basis for the curriculum in the classroom, for debate, and for heightening students' awareness toward the issues of racism, homophobia, and prejudice.
   - With a partner, identify a number of ways to design inter-disciplinary curriculum units that deal with these issues and other sensitive issues you have encountered in classrooms and schools.
   - Organize a series of roundtables where colleagues can share creative ideas, lesson plans, and curriculum units that address issues of equity, difference, diversity, and justice.
   - Find a way of publicly displaying the materials generated.

9. John's narrative provides insights into one teacher's efforts to challenge the "taken-for-granteds" in his life. Use the following questions to question the "official stories" and taken-for-granteds in your professional situations.
   - Whose knowledge is of value here?
   - Whose values, voices, and belief systems are important?
   - Who benefits from the system as it is currently organized and enacted?

- Who is disadvantaged by the structures, systems, relationships, and ways of being that are enacted in the professional situation you have chosen to examine?
10. John's essay provides a new narrative of teacher leadership. It is a story of a beginning teacher who collaborates with the associate teacher and the principal of the school to confront challenges and to act in ways that are compassionate, caring and creative. By joining forces, these professionals support each other and share the responsibility for the maintenance of a just and caring learning community.
    - Recall an incident from your own experience in schools where this kind of leadership—people joining hands and leading together—was in evidence.
    - Describe the learning community in which this took place and any observations you might have about the ways in which this kind of leadership affected classroom practices and students' lives.
    - Describe the ways in which you think shared leadership would improve the cultures of schools and the quality of students' experiences in classrooms and schools.

CHAPTER 12

Creating Community: Seeking Common Ground

My fullest concentration of energy is available only when I integrate all the parts of who I am, openly, allowing power from particular sources of my living to flow back and forth freely through all my different selves, without the restrictions of externally imposed definition. Only then can I bring myself and my energies as a whole to the service of those struggles which I embrace as part of my living.

AUDRE LORDE

Ruth Weinstock's narrative focuses on the image of the teacher as community builder, team member, and visionary. Ruth describes the artistry involved in weaving disparate elements together, finding common ground with others, and creating shared understandings, values, and meanings. Her narrative illustrates how one prospective teacher understands the need to rescript the story of teacher-student relationships, of classrooms and schools as she knows them, and to translate her vision into practical actions. It shows her recognition of the temporal nature of structures, procedures, and ways of being. She envisions and enacts a script for classroom and school communities that is based on "relationships and relevance . . . and that balances the human need for interdependence with respect for individual difference."

Ruth's narrative provides insights into her philosophy of teaching and learning, a philosophy that presents her image of the teacher as a leader in the maintenance of "a moral universe." Relationships and connections between people and things are at the heart of her understanding of the teacher's role. She describes this role as the creation of opportunities for student success, for capacity building, and for the development of the whole person. Here, student engagement and motivation are attained through authentic relationships, not through coercion or manipulation.

Ruth portrays the teacher as a team member engaged in shared leadership, working continually to build relationships with students and colleagues, connecting her personal vision with that of others and collaborating with others to bring about positive change. She describes the ways in which she shares ideas and insights, observes and gauges others' needs and desires, works to find the intersection between disparate groups' purposes and values, and shares decision making and resources. Ruth's narrative presents a portrait of a teacher who is a relationship builder, community maker and creator of a new script for teachers, classrooms, schools, and learning communities.

Riding the Waves: Learning to Adapt

by Ruth Weinstock

I have never actually gone surfing, but the constantly shifting environment I lived in taught me, early on, to adapt and "ride the waves."

I am a middle child, one of three. My two sisters are 6 years apart, which meant that at various times in their development they were at odds with each other and, at other times, they were the best of friends.

When they were at loggerheads, my mother would sometimes use me as the buffer zone between them. If we were in the car, I would be seated in the middle to prevent tiffs. My middle position in the family has shaped my perspective, my values, and the roles I have undertaken in life.

As a child, I became willy-nilly, a peacemaker, a negotiator, a meeting ground between two very different and very strong personalities. I learned to adapt to the expectations of two very different sisterly playmates and a feeling that the sands were always shifting, a feeling of not being in control of my world. Unsure of myself and unaware of what other role I might have chosen if given the choice, I became not so much an actor, initiating events, but a responder to set circumstances. I learned to listen, to have my antennae operating at all times, to observe, and to gauge my response to what was needed "out there." I have never actually gone surfing, but the constantly shifting environment I lived in taught me, early on, to adapt and "ride the waves."

I have felt over and over again in my life the influence of this early training in joining disparate elements at odds with one another and finding common ground. Maybe it is no accident that the art processes I am most attracted to involve collage. If there is a key metaphor in my life, it would probably be weaving, a joining together of warp and woof into one fabric.

The Teacher as Matchmaker: Seeking Common Ground

*My conscious approach to community building is one of the
strengths I have as a teacher, because I strive to balance the human
needs for interdependence with respect for individual differences.*

In the late 1970s I was hired as publicity manager of Harbourfront,
a cultural-recreation center on Toronto's waterfront. Because I had no
extensive prior experience doing publicity, I adopted a working approach
based on what I knew best. I felt my task was to find some common ground
between the programs Harbourfront had to offer and the subject matter
radio and TV producers and newspaper writers were willing to cover. To
me, my work was a game of matchmaking, bringing together the media's
need for a good story with our need for inexpensive public awareness.

I pictured my work in terms of a Venn diagram—a matter of finding
where the media's purpose and Harbourfront's purpose, though disparate,
could intersect. The image of the Venn diagram, the seeking of common
ground, is one I have found useful and applicable in many personal and
professional situations. It can be seen as a metaphor for the creation of a
community, and it is one of the first tasks I undertake as a teacher when I meet
with the diverse group of individuals who will become "my" class. In this way,
differences can be respected, but the people in the class can also spend time
together with a profound sense of common purpose. My conscious approach
to community building is one of the strengths I have as a teacher, because
I strive to balance the human needs for interdependence with respect for
individual differences.

Many aspects of the experience at Harbourfront prepared me for life
as a teacher. Harbourfront then was an organization made up of many
different departments—from development to dance, from a school of urban
studies to a department sponsoring ethnic events. Each department felt its
activities were worthy of media coverage, and each one demanded attention, just as students in a class do. At the end of my first year there, I was
asked to write a description of my job for an evaluation. I realized that the
key words that defined my job were *relationships* and *relevance*. To glean
the information essential for my work, I needed to form relationships with
and gain the trust of a broad spectrum of my coworkers, all of whom had
their own disparate agendas. I also had to assimilate and summarize
mountains of information quickly, select key items, and be able to demonstrate their relevance to a highly skeptical and resistant media audience.
I had to convince the media, over a period of time, that I understood what
they were all about and that my judgment could be trusted, just as
the teacher must daily build relationships in a classroom and make the
material relevant to her students.

Thus, my work put me in the middle, between my colleagues at
Harbourfront on the one side and the media on the other. It demanded of me

the same skills of listening and mediation that I had acquired in the backseat of my parents' car years before.

There are further parallels between my publicity work and the demands of teaching. I learned to multitrack on a grand scale. I constantly read, listened to, and watched all the local, national, and international media one human possibly could to be aware of the current preoccupations of writers and producers. There are wide differences in the needs and approaches of each media outlet. I had to learn to employ *Globe and Mail* English in one conversation and switch to the *Sun* in the next. I developed the habit of automatically adjusting my pace, level of language, and complexity of concepts, depending on my media audience. I learned to expand or contract what I had to say, depending on how much time the media had available, to think on my feet and to counter resistance. During my practice teaching sessions in high school, I learned to draw on all of these skills to meet students' needs in multilevel classrooms.

I have also learned to juggle a constantly shifting agenda of priorities, to meet deadlines despite constant interruptions, and to take care of the inevitable problems, surprises, and upsets. Though I personally needed to feel in control of events in the classroom, I learned that I had to let go of this need to some degree and learn to ride the waves, or I would have gone crazy.

Queen of the Funny Tangent, Queen of Control

> *It never occurred to me that planning this tightly, and praying that nothing spontaneous would upset my neat and ordered plans, meant that I was rehearsing and predetermining life before it was lived.*

Though I wasn't aware of the tension between control and creativity in my life when I was at Harbourfront, I became increasingly aware of it when, several years later in 1988, I began to teach for the institution now called Ryerson Polytechnic University.

My very first teaching experience had taken place about 25 years earlier, teaching arts and crafts on Saturday mornings. Although I don't have a clear memory of those classes, they doubtless met the standards of teaching favored then—classes in which students were led, step-by-step, in how-to activities instead of discovering on their own what they could and wished to do.

The first taste I had of teaching creatively came at the age of 18, when I began teaching creative writing to gifted children on Saturdays, which I did off and on for 6 years. I remember one class in which I brought a bag of fabrics of various textures and patterns. I sat down on the floor with the children, picked out a piece of black-and-white striped fabric, and started making up the story of a zebra who took off his clothes and laid them on a riverbank while he went swimming on a very hot day. Then I passed the bag around and each child took a piece of fabric out, transformed its texture into a personality, and launched the most delightful stories.

Teaching creative writing was the best job I had ever had and one of the most exciting, open-ended experiences of my life. I would come in full of ideas, listen to theirs, and let the kids carry us in any freewheeling direction that beckoned. I never knew what was going to happen until the class was over. I loved it. The kids, who only signed up for the classes they wanted, loved it. Later on, I gave the workshops to teachers in how to teach creative writing and realized I prepared for my teaching, in part, by simply believing in and visualizing the kids writing creatively.

It frustrated me to realize that some teachers saw me as some kind of special creative genie, able to do something that was beyond them. I believed that anyone could inspire creativity if they gave themselves permission to let go. I went on to get a grant to write a book on how to teach creative writing and spent hours in the Ontario Institute for Studies in Education (OISE) Library, reading and researching creativity.

About 20 years later, I began to teach at Ryerson. In my first year there, it never occurred to me to take a lesson from the open-ended approach I had used in teaching creative writing. This was a serious university. I should lecture. I prepared voluminous notes. I read reams of references. I went in armored. In control. To be a student in my class that year was to receive a course outline on the first day and to know exactly what we had covered each step of the way. Classes operated on what I would call the "transfer" theory of education. I had the knowledge, and if I talked fast enough and made enough lists, I could "pour" it into the students' minds. Everything was tightly structured, organized, and planned to the hilt. It never occurred to me that this was like eating the same fish dinner with the same sauce every Wednesday and the same chicken recipe every Friday. It never occurred to me that planning this tightly, and praying that nothing spontaneous would upset my neat and ordered plans, meant that I was rehearsing and predetermining life before it was lived.

Then, into my tightly planned first-year Ryerson class stepped a clown, a gadfly, the class bad-ass. If and when he came, he neatly derailed and chopped into bits my carefully prepared lesson plans. He constantly sidetracked us with his questions, his sassing, his humor, his politically incorrect views, intended to raise any remaining righteous hackles. Some of the students couldn't stand his attention-getting tactics. I loved him for stirring us up. Maybe he spread the word about my class, because into the next year came several of his friends. By this time I had relaxed a little and had begun to let the students have more control in the class. The fact that I had loosened up a bit was reflected in one evaluation I received at the end of this second year. The evaluation took the form of a cartoon, a picture of me labeled "Queen of the Funny Tangent" in recognition of the butterfly side of my nature.

Joining the Warp and the Woof: Weaving a Philosophy of Teaching

I began to feel that I had talent as a facilitator, someone who would make things happen and not just respond to events.

Between my time at Harbourfront and my years at Ryerson, I began to work at the Royal Ontario Museum where the theme was weaving. At the time, there were six different unions at the museum; two of them had just come back to work after a bitter strike. The new director, attempting to heal rifts, created a liaison committee in which union heads and management could discuss and address outstanding issues. Because I was not part of the "old guard," I didn't feel jaded or demoralized. My appointment to this committee gave me experience in attempting to negotiate systemwide changes with a group of people who were angry and far from ready to believe that change was possible. It was one of a number of experiences I have had with people who seem to want a platform on which they can complain about the past and aren't yet fully ready to visualize the future, a situation somewhat akin to the response some teachers may have to school restructuring and to change initiatives. I found myself then, and still find myself today, willing to put up with only a certain amount of "awfulizing." I get impatient when complaints are used as a means of staving off the exciting work of finding solutions.

It was at the museum that I began to feel I had talent as a facilitator, someone who would make things happen and not just respond to events. I had always been tenacious and able to picture solutions, but I lacked confidence in myself and my convictions and the assertiveness to make things happen. I would back off and not press my case in a confrontation, afraid to lose approval and jeopardize relationships. A turning point came for me when the museum was called on to host an exhibition called "The Precious Legacy." It was a collection of artifacts from Jewish homes, museums, and synagogues stolen by the Nazis in Czechoslovakia and intended to be shown in a macabre "museum to a vanished race." The art writer for a large-circulation newspaper agreed to write a story about the artifacts but refused to write a second, human interest story based on interviews with two Torontonians originally from Czechoslovakia who had somehow managed to survive this tragedy. It was an unwritten rule that no single exhibition merited two stories. I was infuriated.

Knowing it could cost me my job and would certainly earn me the enmity of the art writer on whom I depended for regular coverage, I deluged the senior management of the paper with letters, insisting on a second story. I got my story, learned to live with having an enemy, and connected with a kind of fire or anger in me that is aroused when my idea of a moral order in the universe is violated.

Getting Angry: Defending Communal Ideals in the Classroom

Teachers must be part of creating and maintaining a moral universe.

I reexperienced this same bulldog anger when, as a student teacher, in a practice teaching situation, I saw a wrong that needed righting. A young girl ran up to me in class after the bell rang, excitedly telling me that she had changed her mind about the book she was going to read, as she had found a new and more wonderful one. I gave her my full attention, not realizing that while we were in conversation, her extremely expensive calculator was being swiped. A second later, on going to her desk and realizing it was missing, she was in hysterics. She was terrified of repercussions from her father, whom I later was told was a judgmental and difficult man. She also was, quite obviously, very poor. The calculator had not been purchased without some thought, other teachers in the department said.

The girl immediately began to accuse the boy who sat behind her, whom I'll call Fred. Fred rarely came to class, but when he did, he displayed an anger and callousness toward other humans that was chilling. When faced with moral dilemmas in literary excerpts, he laughed at others' desire to protect the infirm and elderly. In answer to the question "What are basic human needs?" others had listed "food and shelter." Fred's answer? "Murder." It's true that some kids would say this only to shock and get attention; few would say this with cold-blooded conviction. My guts told me that Fred might be in the latter group.

Fred had quickly disappeared down the hall, surrounded by a swarm of classmates. I called out after him, and he hesitated. It was too far away for me to see, but it was within the realm of possibility that before returning to me, Fred had passed the calculator to one of his friends. My associate appeared, and, with the victimized girl bleating out accusations, we asked Fred into the department office to empty out his pockets and bags. A male teacher who knew Fred well joined us.

Fred kept up a steady stream of patter, some of it ingratiating, some of it vituperative, while he emptied out his pockets and emptied his bag. Chattering nonstop, he also gave us a detailed dissertation on how to steal successfully and fence stolen school property and explained why, in this case, he had clearly departed from these "rules" and therefore was innocent. His argument ran back and forth from one idea to the next like a ricocheting pinball.

I listened to this stream of alternating viciousness and charm and saw a classic con man. We were being had. I couldn't believe my ears when the two teachers on staff soft-pedaled every word they said to him. While it was clearly unwise to accuse Fred without any evidence, they obviously felt helpless in pushing their case, even to the extent of being reluctant to ask him to "help" them find the calculator by asking around. Their softness infuriated me, and I found myself taking a much harder tone with Fred than they did. The other teachers seemed almost horrified that I would do this. On reflection, I realize they were stuck with Fred, whereas my contact with him would end in 2 weeks when my practice session was over and I could return to the safe haven provided by being a student. What brought our altercation to an end was Fred's taunt "What are you going to do—call the police? They won't come, not for a calculator." I could see he was right. We had to let him go. The system was stacked in favor of the Freds of the world.

After Fred had gone, I urged his regular classroom teacher not to ignore the incident, but to assume that knowledge of the theft would travel in class. Could he address the kids on the subject of the sheer immorality of aiding and abetting criminal activity? I felt, at the very least, this would support the victim and also be seen as an act of openness, rather than glossing over a difficult situation. At first he wasn't thrilled at the idea of opening a can of worms, but he eventually agreed and did a wonderful job the next day of stating the case for ethical behavior.

Later in the week, another class ended, ironically, with Fred bellowing that someone had stolen his hat. I prevented the class from leaving until the missing hat was returned. I told Fred that he, like everyone else who had something stolen, deserved equal treatment and a chance to get his property back, hoping he would learn something now that the tables were turned. He did get his hat back and swiftly termed the theft a "joke." The incident left me fairly certain that he had not learned anything and the calculator had still not been returned by the time I left the school.

In discussing my evaluation, my associate remarked on and complimented me for getting angry, as prior to this she had believed I was "soft-spoken" and, perhaps, also soft in nature. To me, teachers must be part of creating and maintaining a moral universe, one in which the bad guys do not triumph and in which most kids have a fair chance. It makes me livid to think that, without intending it, teachers could be passively allowing an ethical universe to disappear inch by inch, leaving those students who want to go by the rules to fend for themselves, without our support.

The Teacher as Community Maker

> *Dogmatic thinking raises my hackles; certainty and closed-mindedness scare me.*

I find myself given to seeking explanations, looking behind systems at the assumptions that they are built on. I often question, examine, and reflect on the subtext of what humans say and do. I am interested in how all things human come to be the way they are and how it is possible to engender change and growth, for I do not accept that the way things are is the way they must be.

My nature may lead me in two conflicting directions, but it also leads me to try to find ways to make sense of these opposites and integrate them. I find myself able to step back and "see," if not accept, both sides of an argument and to entertain many points of view, traits that I've found very useful in teaching. This does not mean I operate without an ethical base. Nor does it mean that I cannot make decisions (although, admittedly, some decisions come hard). It simply means that one of the tenets of my morality is a thoroughgoing mistrust of dogma.

This last statement is exceedingly important to me. Dogma is an anathema to me. Dogmatic thinking raises my hackles; certainty and closed-mindedness scare me. I mistrust doctrinaire research that "proves" that we ought to teach using X or Y approach. Experience shows that over the years, one orthodoxy or another, one set of assumptions, beliefs, trends, and "truths," has been supplanted by other "truths." What is newest isn't necessarily better for the individuals in my class or for me. The best gift I can give my students is to continue to enlarge my perspective as a human and to maintain my belief in both/and over either/or thinking. In seeking to be this kind of human being, I find that my students will be my best teachers.

Several days ago, a friend posed a question to me. What would I do if I were in the ocean, swimming to shore, and found not a shoreline but a big black wall rising above the sea? I pictured myself swimming and searching, feeling cold, seeing the looming wall blocking out the horizon and eliminating possibility. Then my picture changed. Around a bend, the wall crumbled, and there was a hospitable shoreline. I know that when I keep on looking, I always find a way. When I ask myself about what is really important to me as a teacher, this is what I tell myself. Yes, I am task oriented, an achiever. Yes, getting things done and being productive is central to my being. Yes, it's true that I don't know what to do tomorrow unless I follow the (lengthy) list I made today. However, there is another side to my nature just as assertively demanding airtime. I am drawn to creative work in art, writing, and music and, especially, to creative people. What really makes me know in my gut that I am creative are the ideas that stream into my brain constantly, spouting and flowing over each other, whether I have time to develop them or not. Sometimes I can't help myself but must flit after them, arguing with my "control" side, which wants to keep me productive, goal oriented, and on track.

Lessons to Live By

- Think about what "community" means to you. You have the opportunity to build a community.
- Think of your classroom as a crossroads. Connect your students to individuals and institutions in the world.
- Find out what your students have in common with each other and you.
- Think intergenerationally. Seniors are an unimaginable resource.

- Create rituals because of the rhythm, peace, and pleasure they add to life.
- Laugh together: Use comic strips, jokes, games, and icebreakers.

Reflecting, Responding, and Writing

1. Respond to Ruth's narrative by identifying those aspects of her story that have significant meaning for you. Explain the significance of her narrative in the context of your own efforts to establish a community of learners in your classroom.
2. The theme of control and creativity provides a way for Ruth to explore the moral purpose of her teaching. Describe the moral purpose at the heart of your teaching. How do you work toward the enactment of this in your practice?
   - What obstacles do you experience in doing so?
   - Describe any successes you have had in overcoming these obstacles.
   - Discuss these issues and ideas with your colleagues, and document the discussions.
3. Describe your understanding of Ruth's discussion of teacher leadership.
   - Explain how you take up leadership roles in your personal and professional lives. Describe your style of leadership.
   - Share your writing with a colleague, and discuss the implications of your conceptions of leadership for your work in schools and in the profession.
   - Organize a panel discussion on this topic where individuals with different perspectives offer their conceptions of leadership, and discuss the implications of these for the future of teachers, of schools, and of the profession.
4. The kind of teaching and leadership that Ruth describes requires sophisticated levels of teaching and leadership, negotiating, gauging others' needs and desires, observing, mediating, facilitating, building relationships and community, and communicating. The development of these skills and competencies is a lifelong commitment.
   - Make a plan for your own long-term professional development based on your current position. Identify the indicators you will use to assess growth in each of these areas.
   - Identify the obstacles you perceive to the achievement of your goals.

- Describe the benefits you see in the full achievement of your goals.
- Describe the resources, support, experiences, and conditions that would help you to achieve these goals.
- Make a plan for professional development by mapping out the journey that will enable you to become the teacher you want to be.

5. Interview teachers whose leadership you admire. Ask them about their work as teacher-leaders. Share your findings with a colleague.

6. Describe what you have learned from the narratives in this section by Jana, John, and Ruth. Document your reflections. Share your reflections with a colleague, and discuss ways to incorporate new ideas into your existing practice.

7. Listening to others and adapting understandings and practices in light of new insights and perspectives are strong themes throughout the narratives in this section. Reflect on the ways in which you plan to develop your capacities in this regard. Describe the benefits of collegiality, collaboration, and a strong support system in the context of your professional learning. Share your written reflections with a colleague.

8. Jana, John, and Ruth reframe the stories they have inherited about teacher-student relationships, classroom practices, collegial relations, and school cultures. They struggle to enact new narratives that will enable them to live their professional lives as ethically based practitioners.
   - Describe your plans for your career ahead. Be idealistic and enthusiastic, for, in the words of Ralph Waldo Emerson (2003), "Nothing great was ever achieved without enthusiasm" (p. 324).
   - Share your plans with colleagues. Discuss the obstacles you may encounter and ways to overcome them. Describe the benefits of being true to yourself and of living a professional life that is in harmony with your beliefs, morals, goals, and vision as a teacher.
   - Make a plan for your professional development, review it regularly, and use your ongoing planning and inquiry to become the person and the professional you want to be.

CHAPTER 13

Writing a Narrative

Composing a life involves a continual reimagining of the future and reinterpretation of the past to give meaning to the present, remembering best those events that prefigured what followed, forgetting those that proved to have no meaning within the narrative.

M. C. BATESON

Writing a narrative will involve you in describing your journey of professional learning and show the ways in which you have constructed and reconstructed your professional knowledge through reflection and inquiry. The narrative you create will be a historical document—a snapshot in time—that will present your knowledge and perspectives in a way that is as unique as the person and professional you are. As you weave the threads of seemingly disparate events together into a coherent whole, you will be creating a self-portrait that is temporal and that will change as you develop new knowledge and understandings. You will return to this narrative at many times during your professional career as you continue to engage in inquiry and to create new narratives.

Writing the narrative is a continuation of the inquiry process, and the writing itself will involve you in further reflection, interpretation, and application to practice and in making connections between experiences and ideas. As you reflect back on the learning and unlearning you have done, and on the significant events and surprising turns in your life's journey so far, you will find that the reflective writing you have done in your portfolio will be an excellent resource for you. It will help you to make links between the continuities of your past, your emerging future, and the present you are enacting. As you draw on this excellent resource material, you will develop the courage to further explore the interior of your being and to dig deep into your memories—those memories that

Faith is a bird that feels dawn breaking and sings while it is still dark

have formed you and those you have inherited from the dreams of your ancestors. Use the writing to express how history, dreams, and realities have interacted in your life and have created the structures within which you have made decisions and directed the flow of your life. Listen to what a character in Ben Okri's (1995) novel *Astonishing the Gods* says about the way dreams and fate interact:

> "Fate is strange," she mused. We plan our lives according to a dream that came to us in our childhood, and we find that life alters our plans. And yet, at the end, from a rare height, we also see that our dream was our fate. It's just that providence had other ideas as to how we would get there. Destiny plans a different route, or turns the dream around, as if it were a riddle, and fulfills the dream in ways we wouldn't have expected. How far back is our childhood? Twenty years? Thirty? Fifty? Or ten? I think our childhood goes back thousands of years, farther back than the memory of any race. When we yearn, our yearning comes through from deep below. It comes from a deep remembering, from the forgotten dreams of our mingled ancestry. (pp. 113–114)

Writing your narrative will help you to make your tacit knowledge explicit, to articulate the various dimensions of your professional knowledge, and to use what you know to learn what you need to know. It will help you to express the central concerns and values in your life, to explore how they are enacted in your professional practice, and to imagine and create the script for your future life.

MAPPING OUT THE JOURNEY

Faith is a bird that feels dawn breaking and sings while it is still dark.

Scandinavian saying

Prewriting

Read through the writing you have done in your professional portfolio, and reflect on the ways in which you have learned from the rich set of experiences you have encountered throughout your life's journey. Make some notes of your findings.

Reread the narratives written by the beginning teachers in the text, and think about the issues that they identify as significant to them. Reflect on the similarities and differences between your experiences and those described in the narratives in the book. Look at how each individual has presented his or her narrative, and think about how you will present yours. Again, make some notes of your reflections.

Read over the entire body of your own writing again, looking for the clusters of ideas, stories, and the patterns you find emerging from the writing. Look also for the tensions, inconsistencies, irregularities, and seemingly disconnected or surprising issues and ideas you find in the writing. Make some notes about your findings.

Write a set of "Lessons to Live By" (see chapter 2 for an example). This will help you to clarify what is important to you in your life, in your teaching practices, and in your professional career.

Classifying and Coding

Begin to classify the writing by sorting the stories, reflections, and ideas into groups or clusters. As you begin to see the themes or clusters emerging from the writing, give each of these emergent groupings a name or a symbol to identify it. Begin by looking for the stories and accounts of the *major events* of your life history, the experiences and stories that have *shaped* your life, the things you *love*, the memories that *sustain* you, the *consistencies and continuities* in your life, and the *people* who are most important to you in your personal and professional lives. Look closely at any writing that shows *significant emotional content*, and probe this deeply for its meanings. Find places in the writing where you have written about *changes to your knowledge, skills and ways of being*. Look for stories of *learning* and *unlearning*. Look also for *tensions, inconsistencies*, and *paradoxes* in the writing.

Search carefully for the stories and accounts of practice that tell of the *creation of a professional identity*, the *creation of relationships with students and colleagues*, and the *connections among yourself, the school, and the community*.

Use the following suggestions to help you as you classify and code and work to identify the *major themes, subthemes,* and *tensions* in your writing. Look for these elements:

- The metaphors, similes, images, descriptions, and stories that provide insights into what you know and can do in your professional practice
- Any recurring patterns in your actions and practices over time, and examples of consistencies throughout your life's journey—those qualities, patterns, and themes that have remained the same in your life regardless of all else
- Examples of important sources of meaning and satisfaction in your life. Look especially for those nonmaterial aspects of life that provide you with nourishment and rewards.
- Examples of unlearning and/or of significant changes that have taken place in your thinking and in your way of being over time
- Things you are passionate about
- Changes in the way you talk about yourself as a teacher
- Stories that show the development of self-esteem, self-confidence, and a sense of competence as a teacher
- Stories that illustrate the development of your ability to express your ideas, opinions, and understandings
- Growth in the intellectual, emotional, social, spiritual, moral, and aesthetic dimensions of your life
- Changes in your relationship to knowledge (Do you see any differences in your understanding about who has the authority to make knowledge? Do you see any differences in your understanding of the role of the teacher, the student, the curriculum, and the classroom with regard to the making of knowledge in schools?)
- Changes in your relationship to the subjects you teach (Do you notice any differences in the way you relate to subject disciplines? Have you made any changes to the content of the curriculum you teach? Is your teaching any more or less teacher-directed or student-centered than it was at another time?)
- Changes in the ways you set up your classroom as a learning environment (Does your classroom have visual, aural, aesthetic, or physical dimensions that it did not have in the past?)
- Changes in the way you relate to students in the classroom and in extracurricular contexts
- Changes in your ability to communicate with students, to hear them on their own terms, to acknowledge their realities and ways of being in the world
- Changes in your ability to respond to what students tell you and to adapt your teaching to enhance their learning

- Changes in the way you relate to colleagues, parents, and others in educational settings
- Growth in your ability to make connections between your work, students' self-development, and positive change in schools
- Stories about your attempts to make connections between your own work, the interests of others, and larger social and global issues

CHARTING THE JOURNEY OF PROFESSIONAL LEARNING

- Represent your findings visually as a thought web, a map, or a chart of the professional landscape of your life. Look at how the themes you have identified are related to the themes of the text, and use these themes to structure your writing or create new ones. Some possible themes are: Creating a professional identity: connecting the personal and the professional: creating relationships and making new relations: learning from and with others; and creating new narratives: connecting self, school, and society. Some of your writing will not fit neatly into a theme, and it is likely that there will be overlap between themes. At this stage, place the writing in the thematic category that is the closest fit.

Creating a Professional Identity

- Personal strengths, skills, knowledge
- Connecting the personal and the professional
- Personal attributes
  - Intellectual
  - Social
  - Moral
  - Aesthetic
  - Spiritual
  - Cultural

Creating a Personal Narrative

Creating New Narratives for Self, School, and Society

- Creating a democratic classroom
- Creating collegial, collaborative relationships with colleagues and parents
- Connecting to networks for making positive changes for schools and society

Creating Relationships

- Creating respectful, caring relationships with students
- Creating a cohesive, collaborative classroom community
- Learning from and with others
- Learning about students' interests, purposes, ways of learning
  - Making new relations between ideas, insights, understandings
- Building relationships of respect, trust, and reciprocity with colleagues, parents, school administration, education officials, and community members

CREATING A PERSONAL NARRATIVE

- Write on each of the major themes you have identified, supporting what you say with stories, accounts of practice, and quotes from your reflective writing.
- Enjoy the writing; hold back your inner critic. Remember that this draft of the narrative will be reshaped and re-formed at the next stage, so let the writing flow. Be flexible, be loose, let go, and write the first draft.
- Look at what you have written on each of the themes separately. Identify the ways in which the themes overlap and intersect with each other. Make the connections between them, and think about how to rearrange the material to take account of these connections. You may want to move material from one section to another at this point.
- Use subheadings and suitable titles to provide an internal framework for your writing. Your subheadings will help a reader to understand how a particular section of the writing relates to the whole narrative.
- Write another draft of the narrative.
- Share this draft orally with a trusted colleague by telling your colleague how you are presenting your narrative, the major themes you are using to structure the piece, the tensions you have identified within the themes, and the headings and subheadings you will use to structure the writing. Ask for an oral response and constructive feedback. Make notes that you can consider and possibly use, as you prepare to write the next draft.

RESPONDING TO YOUR OWN WRITING

Consider the following questions and the responses you have received from your colleague as you read over what you have written. Make the necessary notes and marks on the text as you read and respond to these questions. Write another draft of the text.

- Does the narrative give an authentic account of the experiences you have had as a person and as a prospective teacher?
- Does the narrative provide insights and understandings into the actual experiences of becoming a teacher and of learning to teach (the ups and downs, the dilemmas, the joys and difficulties, the triumphs and failures, the frustrations, the inconsistencies, and the nonlinear, nonrational aspects of professional growth)?
- Does the narrative document the processes of professional learning and show the transformation of your understandings and professional knowledge over time?

- Does it show how various theories and perspectives have been incorporated into your professional practice?
- Does the writing have the qualities of coherence, authenticity, integrity, verisimilitude (the ring of truth), and the sense of rightness that true stories display?
- Does the account need the addition of details, clarification of important points, and/or support or additional evidence for ideas or statements made?
- Does the narrative provide insights into these points:
  a. The way you live each day knowing that your own inner life needs nourishment?
  b. The way you use your special gifts to make a positive difference in other people's lives?
  c. The way you use your teaching practices to leave the world a little better than you found it?
- Is the narrative account coherent and well written?
- Is it well structured, with a clear beginning, middle, and end?
- Is the writing free of jargon or impenetrable language?
- Can your unique voice be heard in the writing?

GETTING A RESPONSE FROM A READER

When you have written the necessary drafts of your narrative to feel that you have given it your best effort, have a trusted partner read and respond to it. Using the reader-response questions given here, ask your partner to respond in writing with as much detail as possible. Before you write another draft, you will consider all these suggestions. Having done this, you will make your own judgments regarding how you will write the next draft.

Coherence of the Account

- Does the account have a coherent structure/contours/a shape? What is it? Describe the structure or shape as you see it.
- How could the structure be improved? Provide suggestions for improvement (such as alternate structures, sectioning, headings, and use of subheads and quotations).

Evidence of Reflection and Inquiry

- Does the account provide insights into the ways in which the author has experienced his or her professional learning and journey of inquiry?

- Does the account show how the author's professional learning has been influenced by others (teachers, students, parents, policymakers, and theorists)?
- Does the writing show how the author's reflections and thinking have been enacted in practice? Does it provide examples of this application?

Evidence of Professional Insights and Understanding

- Does the account show insights into the author's lived experiences of learning to teach and of becoming a teacher?
- What new ideas, understanding, or questions arose for you as you read the account? Describe.
- What insights into professional learning do you gain from reading the account? Describe what you learned about becoming a teacher.

Reader Response to the Text

- How did you respond to the text? What was its effect on you? What did it cause you to think or feel? Did it enable you to understand and to be a witness to the author's experiences of becoming a teacher?
- Does the account have the qualities of a true story (that is, coherence, integrity, verisimilitude, authenticity, and sense of rightness)?
- Does it resonate for you, the reader, and remind you of things you have experienced, felt, or thought?
- Does it name things you have felt but have not been able to express? Describe them.
- Are any parts of the account incomplete? Are there parts where you wished you had more information, more descriptive detail, more evidence provided for a statement made? Identify these, and provide as much detail as possible regarding what needs to be added.
- Are there parts of the account where you felt you were given too much detail, irrelevant details, or distracting details? Identify the parts that you think should be omitted.
- How do you think this narrative could be improved for a potential reader? Make some suggestions for improvement.

WRITING A FINAL DRAFT: DOCUMENTING THE JOURNEY OF PROFESSIONAL LEARNING

Choose a form for your narrative that enables you to present the journey of your professional learning through reflection and inquiry. You might choose a form similar to one used in the chapters here, or you may want to create something new. As Maxine Greene (1995) has said, "Learning to write is a matter of learning to shatter the silences, of making meaning, of learning to learn" (p. 108). Now, as you write, consider the following:

- What is my purpose?
- Who is my audience?
- What stories and details are at the foreground, and what stories and details need to be in the background?
- What insights and understandings about the learning journey do I especially want to present?
- What feelings, insights, and understandings do I want my reader to have?

Begin your final draft when you are satisfied that you have made final decisions about the content, structure, language use, style, and form of your narrative. Taking all the feedback you have received into account, remember that you are the author, and you have the authority to write it in the way you choose. Your final narrative will be presented through your unique sensibilities, your ways of seeing and making sense of the world, and your perspectives on learning and on life. It will be as unique as your signature or the sound of your voice. It will reflect your humanity and the professional teacher you are at this point in time. Enjoy the opportunity to create a work that shows the realities of your lived experience and your journey of professional learning.

CHAPTER 14

Contributing to the Existing Literature

Centuries after we are dead,
cities shall be overthrown,
it may be because of an
air that we have hummed
or because of a curtain
full of meaning that we
have hung upon a wall.

W. B. YEATS

Practitioner research is a vibrant and expanding aspect of educational research that emphasizes *reflection* and *inquiry* in the process of becoming a teacher, improving professional practice and students' learning, and making a positive difference in school and social settings. The various traditions of practitioner research—action research, teacher research, self-study research, and narrative and autobiographical research—are outlined by Zeichner and Noffke (2001) in the *Handbook of Research on Teaching* and by Cochran-Smith and Lytle (2004) in the *International Handbook of Self-Study in Teaching and Teacher Education Practices*. Although these lines of inquiry have their own distinctive features, the reasons people engage themselves or are engaged by others in this kind of research are understood as "ranging from an interest in understanding one's own students and improving one's own teaching, to generating knowledge about teaching and schooling that can be shared with others, to improving the various social and institutional contexts in which their educational practice is embedded" (Zeichner and Noffke, 2001, p. 323).

Rewriting the stories of self, school, and society

In narrative inquiry, as in other forms of practitioner research, the voices and perspectives of teachers can be heard in the arena of educational research. This kind of research allows practitioners to describe the ways in which they experience their learning—the difficulties of it, the joys of it and the complexities of it. The connections among the individual's past experiences, current situations, and future purposes and goals are acknowledged, as also is the interconnectedness of the personal and the professional in the individual's life. It is understood that practitioners gain special insights and create new knowledge and understandings when they engage in systematic inquiry into their practices. By engaging in the self-directed inquiry into your experiences in professional learning, as you have throughout these chapters, you have prepared yourself for the ongoing inquiry that will continue throughout your career. This ongoing inquiry will enable you to direct the focus of your professional learning, will enhance your students' learning, and enable you to co-create new scripts for yourself, your students, your school, and society. It will provide you with a context in which to think through issues on an ongoing basis, to engage in continuous self-assessment, and to plan your future actions as an ethically based practitioner.

Narratives written by prospective teachers make a valuable contribution to the existing literature, and connect your voices to the teachers' stories and stories of teachers such as those by Coles (1989), Paley (1981, 1986), Jackson (1968), Ashton-Warner (1963), and Beattie (1995a, 1997a). Your narratives also connect your voices to those of educational researchers whose work is based in narrative inquiry, such as Clandinin

(1986); Connelly and Clandinin (1988); Clandinin and Connelly (2000); Conle (1996); Knowles and Cole (1994); Beattie (1995a, 1995b, 1997a, 1997b, 2004); Christiansen, Goulet, Krentz, and Maeers (1997); and Kitchen (2005). All of this work provides teacher educators and prospective teachers with new possibilities and new ways of understanding professionals' knowledge and ways of knowing. It offers new ways of gaining insights into the complexities of becoming a teacher and of learning to teach. When you write your narrative of professional learning, you are working within the tradition of this existing literature and making your own unique contribution.

The current work on reflective inquiry in learning to teach was established in Dewey's (1916, 1934, 1938a, 1938b) work and in his conceptions of time, space, experience, and sociality, which are central to the family of research on reflective practice. The role of reflection in teacher education and teacher development is central to Schon's (1983, 1987) work on professional knowledge and to the work of researchers such as Schulman (1987), Munby (1986), Munby and Russell (1992), Zeichner (1986), Zeichner and Liston (1987), Smith (1991), Smith and Hatton (1993), and Hatton and Smith (1995). The practices of reflective inquiry in initial teacher education are currently being emphasized in the work of researchers such as Beattie (1997b), Bullough and Gitlin (1995), Craig (1992), Conle (1996), Knowles and Holt-Reynolds (1991), Valli (1992), and Zeichner and Liston (1987, 1990). This approach to teacher education presents the prospective teacher as an active agent in the construction of professional knowledge, recognizes the interconnectedness of the personal and the professional in teachers' lives, and acknowledges the narrative and holistic nature of the processes of teaching, learning, and learning to teach.

Narrative ways of thinking, knowing, and representing what is known have been with us for a long time, and narrative as a form of communication has been with us since the beginning of language. Reaching back to a preliterate oral culture, our ancestors told stories to make sense of the mysteries of their worlds, to pass cultural knowledge on from one generation to another, and to communicate societal norms, values, and shared understanding. Narrative is more than a communication system, it is a mode of thought. It is only in this century that narrative has been recognized and acknowledged as a way of thinking and as a fundamental way that individuals structure their experience and make sense of their worlds. As Bruner (1986) explains, we construct ourselves through narrative and make sense of our lives by telling stories of those lives.

Bruner makes a distinction between *paradigmatic* modes of knowing and *narrative* modes of knowing. The former seeks truth; the latter seeks verisimilitude, or observations with the ring of truth. These modes of thinking are used for different purposes. They provide us with different ways of making sense of the world and of responding to the different phenomena in that world—animate and inanimate. Stories provide us with conceptual structures that enable us to store and retrieve knowledge created. They are the structures within which we understand our lives and plan our futures. As Hardy (1968) says, narrative is a way of thinking, a "primary act of mind." We use narrative throughout in our daily lives, for "we not only think in narrative, we also dream in narrative, daydream in narrative, remember, anticipate, hope, despair, believe, doubt, plan, revise, criticize, construct, gossip, learn, hate and love by narrative" (p. 5).

Narrative and story have long been regarded as an intellectual resource in the arts where narrative forms have been used to describe and interpret the experiences of human beings down through the centuries. Narrative is a way of characterizing the phenomenon of human experience, of studying and representing it. The field of study referred to as *narratology* includes such areas as literary theory, drama, film, art, history, theology, linguistics, psychology, anthropology, and education. In narrative inquiry, theory and practice are integrated within an individual's narrative unity of experience, as the individual determines what has significance for him or her in the context of that individual's whole life. This is based on MacIntyre's (1981) concept of a self whose unity resides in the unity of a narrative that links birth to life to death as narrative unites beginning to middle to end.

The philosophical concern with life as narrative involves an emphasis on dialogue, conversation, story, and the processes of inquiry and reflection on experience that allow the individual to identify what has personal significance and meaning for him or her personally. Those processes help to forge a personal vision of reality that takes account of how it was constructed in relation to others, in the context of family and community, and of the social and cultural systems that provide meaning to an individual's existence. Here, theory and practice are connected and integrated in the development of the individual's voice and in the creation of a narrative quest for a better state of things. Personal meanings and understanding are made explicit and placed alongside the concepts, theories, and descriptions of practice that come from others. The narratives we tell and enact show our efforts to determine our places in the world and to direct our lives relative to the good (Taylor, 1989, p. 52). When those narratives are artistically rendered, they can have the power of good literature; they can enable others to enter them imaginatively and to be transformed by them.

Narrative, like literary works of art, has the power to enable others to imagine other ways of being and living. In the telling and the reading, narratives can do what no political tracts, doctrinaire, or explicitly revolutionary material can do. When we read the narratives of teachers and students, we can enter into their experiences, feel as they feel, and interpret and understand as they do. We can experience vicariously how they learn or do not learn. We can hear their voices, their perspectives, and their concerns. We can empathize with them, learn to understand them as they understand themselves, and transcend our own limited experiences and understanding.

Through the narrative representation of people's experiences in learning, we are allowed to catch glimpses of their meaning-making processes and of the frameworks and structures they use to make meanings of their experiences in the contexts of their whole lives. Narratives written by educators allow us to see how they tell, retell, enact, and reenact the stories of themselves, their classrooms, schools, and communities. The power of these narratives lies in their potential to transform and transfigure. Like literature, they show us who we are and who we might become. What matters is our willingness to enter into these stories of professional learning, to interact with the ideas and insights presented there, and to use them to make sense of the stream of events and experiences in our own lives. As ethically based educators, what matters is our willingness to rescript continually the stories of who we are, to challenge and rewrite the stories of school and society, and to create new narratives that are more consistent with a humane, just, and compassionate attitude toward the well-being and development of all human beings.

Ashton-Warner, S. (1963). *Teacher*. New York: Simon & Schuster.

Bateson, M. C. (1989). *Composing a life*. New York: Atlantic Monthly Press.

Beattie, M. (1995a). *Constructing professional knowledge in teaching: A narrative of change and development*. New York: Teachers College Press.

Beattie, M. (1995b, Spring). New prospects for teacher education: Narrative ways of knowing teaching and teacher education. *Educational Research, 37*(1).

Beattie, M. (1997a). Collaboration in the construction of professional knowledge: Finding answers in our own reality. In H. Christiansen, I. Goulet, C. Krentz, & M. Maeers (Eds.), *Recreating relationships: Collaboration and educational reform*. Albany: State University of New York Press.

Beattie, M. (1997b). Fostering reflective practice in teacher education: Inquiry as a framework for the construction of a professional knowledge in teaching. *Asia-Pacific Journal of Teacher Education, 25*(2).

Beattie, M. (2004). *Narratives in the making: Teaching and learning at Corktown Community High School*. Toronto: University of Toronto Press.

Belenky, M., Clinchy, B., Goldberger, N., & Tarule, J. (1986). *Women's ways of knowing*. New York: Basic Books.

Bercheid, E. (1985). Interpersonal modes of knowing. In E. Eisner (Ed.), *Learning and teaching the ways of knowing* (pp. 60–76). Chicago: National Society for the Study of Education.

Bruner, J. (1986). *Actual minds, possible worlds*. Cambridge, MA: Harvard University Press.

Buber, M. (1965). *I and thou* (Ronald G. Smith, Trans.). New York: Scribner's.

Bullough, R. V., & Gitlin, A. (1995). *Becoming a student of teaching*. New York: Garland.

Calderhead, J. (1991). The nature and growth of knowledge in student teaching. *Teaching and Teacher Education, 56*(7), 531–535.

Carter, C., & Doyle, W. (1996). Personal narrative and life history in learning to teach. In *Handbook of research on teacher education* (2nd ed.). New York: Macmillan.

Christiansen, H., Goulet, I., Krentz, C., & Maeers, M. (Eds.). (1997). *Recreating relationships: Collaboration and educational reform*. Albany: State University of New York Press.

Clandinin, J. (1986). *Classroom practice: Teacher images in action*. London: Falmer.

Clandinin, D. J., & Connelly, F. M. (1995). Beginning teaching: Stories of position, and positioning, on the landscape. In D. J. Clandinin & F. M. Connelly (Eds.), *Teachers' professional knowledge landscapes*. New York: Teachers College Press.

Clandinin, D. J., & Connelly, F. M. (1996). Teachers' professional knowledge landscapes. Teacher stories—Stories of teachers—School stories—Stories of schools. *Educational Researcher, 25*(3).

Clandinin, D. J., & Connelly, F. M. (2000). *Narrative inquiry.* San Francisco: Jossey-Bass.

Cochran-Smith, M., & Lytle, S. L. (2004). Practitioner inquiry, knowledge and the university culture. In J. J. Loughran, M. L. Hamilton, V. K. La Boskey, & T. Russell (Eds.), *International handbook of self-study in teaching and teacher education practices* (pp. 602–649). Dordrecht, The Netherlands: Kluwer Academic.

Coles, R. (1989). *The call of stories: Teaching and the moral imagination.* Boston: Houghton Mifflin.

Conle, C. (1996). Resonance in preservice teacher inquiry. *American Educational Research Journal, 33,* 297–325.

Conle, C. (1997). Images of change in narrative inquiry. *Teachers and Teaching: Theory and Practice, 3*(2).

Connelly, F. M., & Clandinin, D. J. (1986). On narrative method, personal philosophy and narrative unities in the story of teaching. *Journal of Research in Science Teaching, 23*(4), 292–310.

Connelly, F. M., & Clandinin, D. J. (1988). *Teachers as curriculum planners: Narratives of experience.* New York: Teachers College Press.

Connelly, F. M., & Clandinin, D. J. (1990). Stories of experience and narrative inquiry. *Educational Researcher, 19*(5), 2–14.

Connelly, F. M., & Clandinin, D. J. (1991). Narrative inquiry: Storied experience. In E. C. Short (Ed.), *Forms of curriculum inquiry: Guidelines for the conduct of educational research* (pp. 121–154). Albany: State University of New York Press.

Connelly, F. M., & Clandinin, D. J. (1993). Reflective practice: Thoughts from the community. *Orbit, 23*(4), 1.

Connelly, F. M., & Clandinin, D. J. (1994). Telling teaching stories. *Teacher Education Quarterly, 21*(2), 145–158.

Connelly, M. Fullan, M., & Watson, N. (1990). *Teacher education in Ontario: Current practice and options for the future.* Toronto: Ontario Ministry of Education.

Craig, C. (1992). *Coming to know in the professional knowledge context: Beginning teachers experiences.* Unpublished doctoral dissertation. University of Alberta, Edmonton.

Dewey, J. (1916). *Democracy in education.* New York: Macmillan.

Dewey, J. (1931). *Philosophy and civilization.* New York: Minton, Balch.

Dewey, J. (1934). *Art as experience.* New York: Capricorn Books.

Dewey, J. (1938a). *Experience and education.* New York: Collier.

Dewey, J. (1938b). *Logic: The theory of inquiry.* New York: Holt.

Dewey, J. (1966). *Democracy and education.* New York: Free Press.

Eisner, E. W. (1985). Aesthetic modes of knowing. In E. W. Eisner (Ed.), *Learning and teaching the ways of knowing* (84th Yearbook of the National Society for the Study of Education, Part 11, pp. 23–36). Chicago: University of Chicago Press.

Eisner, E. W. (2002). *The arts and the creation of mind.* New Haven, CT: Yale University Press.

Elbaz, F. (1983). *Teacher thinking: A study of practical knowledge*. London: Croom Helm.

Emerson, R. (2003). *Selected writings* (W. H. Gilman, Ed.). New York: Signet.

Fenyves, L. (1998, February 20). Paying tribute to an astounding teacher, Christopher Reibling (article writer). *Globe and Mail*, p. C8.

Gilligan, C. (1982). *In a different voice: Psychological theory and women's development*. Cambridge, MA: Harvard University Press.

Goldberg, N. (1986). *Writing down the bones*. Boston: Shambhala.

Goodson, I., & Ball, S. (Eds.). (1985). *Teachers' lives and careers*. London: Falmer.

Greene, M. (1995). *Releasing the imagination*. San Francisco: Jossey-Bass.

Grumet, M. (1987). The politics of personal knowledge. *Curriculum Inquiry, 17*(3).

Hardy, B. (1968). Towards a poetics of fiction: An approach through narrative. *Novel, 2*, 5–14.

Hardy, B. (1975). *Tellers and listeners: The narrative imagination*. London: Athlone.

Hatton, N., & Smith, D. (1995). Reflection in teacher education: Towards definition and implementation. *Teaching and Teacher Education, 11*(1), 33–49.

Heilbrun, C. (1988). *Writing a woman's life*. New York: Ballantine.

Hollingsworth, S. (1992). Learning to teach through collaborative conversation: A feminist approach. *American Educational Research Journal, 229*(2), 373–404.

Huxley, A. (1933). *Texts and pretexts: An anthology with commentaries*. New York: Harper.

Jackson, P. W. (1968). *Life in classrooms*. New York: Holt, Rinehart, & Winston.

Jalongo, M. R., & Isenberg, J. P. (1995). *Teachers' stories: From personal narrative to professional insight*. San Francisco: Jossey-Bass.

Kitchen, J. (2005). *Relational teacher development: A quest for meaning in the garden of teacher experiences*. Unpublished doctoral dissertation, Ontario Institute for Studies in Education at the University of Toronto.

Knowles, G., & Cole, A. (1994). *Through preservice teachers eyes*. New York: Macmillan.

Knowles, G., & Holt-Reynolds, D. (1991). Shaping pedagogies through personal histories in preservice teacher education. *Teachers College Record, 93*(1), 87–113.

Lorde, Audre. (1984). Age, race, class, and sex: Women redefining difference. In *Sister outsider: Essays and speeches*. Trumansburg, NY: Crossing.

MacIntyre, A. (1981). *After virtue: A study in moral theory*. London: Duckworth.

Macmurray, J. (1961). *Persons in relation*. New York: Harper & Row. (Original work published 1954)

McDermott, J. J. (1986). *Streams of experience: Reflections on the history and philosophy of American culture*. Amherst: University of Massachusetts Press.

McIntyre, J. (1998). *Personal and professional renewal: Exploring relational learning among consultants within a group context*. Unpublished doctoral dissertation, University of Toronto.

McLaughlin, D., & Tierney, W. G. (Eds.). (1994). *Naming silenced lives: Personal narratives and the process of educational change*. New York: Routledge.

Merton, T. (1979). *Love and living*. New York: Farrar, Straus & Giroux.

Munby, H. (1986). Metaphor in the thinking of teachers: An exploratory study. *Journal of Curriculum Studies, 18*, 197–209.

Munby, H., & Russell, T. (1996). Transforming research into teaching. In M. Beattie, H. Gruneau, & D. Thiessen (Eds.), *Interpersonal sources of development for beginning and experienced teachers*. Toronto: Among Teachers Community Publication, Ontario Institute for Studies in Education/University of Toronto.

Munby, H., & Russell, T. (Eds.). (1992). *Teachers and teaching: From classroom to reflection.* London: Falmer.

Naylor, G. (1988). *Mama Day.* New York: Ticknor & Fields.

Neill, A. S. (1960). *Summerhill: A radical approach to child rearing.* New York: Simon & Schuster.

Noddings, N. (1984). *Caring: A feminine approach to ethics and moral education.* Berkeley: University of California Press.

Nussbaum, M. (1995). *Poetic justice: The literary imagination and public life.* Boston: Beacon.

Okri, B. (1995). *Astonishing the gods.* Toronto: Little, Brown.

Paley, V. G. (1981). *Wally's stories: Conversations in the kindergarten.* Cambridge, MA: Harvard University Press.

Paley, V. G. (1986). *Molly is three: Growing up in school.* Chicago: University of Chicago Press.

Polanyi, M. (1958). *Personal knowledge.* Chicago: University of Chicago Press.

Schon, D. (1983). *The reflective practitioner: How professionals think in action.* New York: Basic Books.

Schon, D. (1987). *Educating the reflective practitioner.* San Francisco: Jossey-Bass.

Schulman, L. S. (1987). Knowledge and teaching: Foundations of the new reform. *Harvard Educational Review, 57*(1), 1–22.

Smith, D. (1991). Educating the reflective practitioner in curriculum. *Curriculum, 12,* 115–124.

Smith, D., & Hatton, N. (1993). Reflection in teacher education: A study in progress. *Education Research and Perspectives, 20,* 13–23.

Taylor, C. (1989). *Sources of the self.* Cambridge, MA: Harvard University Press.

Thomas, D. (Ed.). (1995). *Teachers' stories.* Buckingham, UK: Open University Press.

Tom, A. (1985). Inquiring into inquiry-oriented teacher education. *Journal of Teacher Education, 36*(5), 35–44.

Valli, L. (1992). *Reflective teacher education: Cases and critiques.* Albany: State University of New York Press.

Vanier, J. (1998). *Becoming human.* New York: Paulist Press

Whitehead, A. N. (1929). *The aims of education and other essays.* New York: Macmillan.

Wilde, O. (1940). The value of art in modern life. In *The best known works of Oscar Wilde, including the poems, novels, plays, essays, and fairy tales.* New York: Halcyon House.

Witherall, C., & Noddings, N. (1991). *Stories lives tell: Narrative and dialogue in education.* New York: Teachers College Press.

Zeichner, K. (1986). Preparing reflective teachers: An overview of instructional strategies which have been employed in preservice teacher education. *International Journal of Educational Research, 11,* 565–575.

Zeichner, K. M., & Liston, D. P. (1987). Teaching student teachers to reflect. *Harvard Educational Review, 57*(1), 23–48.

Zeichner, K. M., & Liston, D. P. (1990). *Traditions of reform and reflective teaching in U.S. teacher education.* East Lansing, MI: National Center for Research in Teacher Education.

Zeichner, K. M., & Noffke, S. E. (2001). Practitioner research. In V. Richardson (Ed.), *Handbook of research on teaching* (pp. 298–332). Washington, DC: American Educational Research Association.